Preferred
Futuring

Preferred Futuring

*Envision the Future You
Want and Unleash the
Energy to Get There*

LAWRENCE L. LIPPITT

Berrett-Koehler Publishers, Inc.
San Francisco

Berrett-Koehler Publishers, Inc.
450 Sansome Street, Suite 1200
San Francisco, CA 94111-3320
Tel: (415) 288-0260   Fax: (415) 362-2512
www.bkpub.com

ORDERING INFORMATION

Individual sales. Berrett-Koehler publications are available through most bookstores. They can also be ordered direct from Berrett-Koehler at the address above.

Quantity sales. Special discounts are available on quantity purchases by corporations, associations, and others. For details, contact the "Special Sales Department" at the Berrett-Koehler address above.

Orders for college textbook/course adoption use. Please contact Berrett-Koehler Publishers at the address above.

Orders by U.S. trade bookstores and wholesalers. Please contact Publishers Group West, 1700 Fourth Street, Berkeley, CA 94710. Tel: 510-528-1444; Fax: 510-528-3444.

Printed in the United States of America

Printed on acid-free and recycled paper that is composed of 50% recycled fiber, including 10% postconsumer waste.

Library of Congress Cataloging-in-Publication Data

Lippitt, Lawrence L., 1941–
      Preferred futuring : envision the future you want and unleash the energy to get there / Lawrence L. Lippitt.—1st ed.
          p.   cm.
      Includes bibliographical references and index.
      ISBN 1-57675-041-8 (alk. paper)
      1. Organizational change. 2. Strategic planning. 3. Problem solving. I. Title.
      HD58.8.L573   1998
      658.4'063—dc21   98-35916
                                                                             CIP

First Edition

02 01 00 99 98   10 9 8 7 6 5 4 3 2 1

Book Production: Pleasant Run Publishing Services
Composition: Classic Typography

Contents

Preface

M any people have come to me and asked where they could be trained in Preferred Futuring or where they could read about Preferred Futuring, so this book is long overdue. It is written for consultants, organizational leaders, managers, or anyone working to stimulate and facilitate change and tap high amounts of empowerment and passion about what we do.

You will not only learn about the Preferred Futuring model and why it works, you will also learn how to use it. The valuable tools included here have been tested and accumulated from decades of my own and others' experiences with using Preferred Futuring. These tools and the accompanying examples show how to stimulate and focus change efforts such as strategic and business planning, mergers, process improvement activities, reengineering, and organization culture change.

The material is divided into four parts. Part One, consisting of the Introduction and Chapters One and Two, first discusses the history of Preferred Futuring, because knowing the roots of the process will provide a deeper understanding and support a more profound use of this process. Part One then previews the eight steps in the Preferred Futuring process and presents some case studies of Preferred Futuring in action.

Part Two, consisting of Chapters Three through Ten, devotes one chapter to each of the eight steps in the process and the tools that can be used to perform each step. Think of these tools as parts of an Erector set, which will be used in Part Three.

Part Three, Chapters Eleven through Fifteen, shows the basic ways of using Preferred Futuring, how to know when to use Preferred Futuring for whole-systems change, and some current variations and applications.

Part Four, Chapters Sixteen and Seventeen, shows how leaders can use Preferred Futuring to make the transition from a hierarchical and autocratic style and organization culture to a participative and democratic style and organization culture. Part Four also shows how to make Preferred Futuring an even more powerful tool. Preferred Futuring becomes more powerful when we understand its connection with our changing view of cause and effect, and when we understand how Preferred Futuring can create healing or wholeness in human systems down to the level of the individual and organizational soul.

This book is for both people familiar with Preferred Futuring and for those who have never heard of it before. It is for people who want to participate in creating their own future.

July 1998   Lawrence L. Lippitt
Ann Arbor, Michigan

Acknowledgments

This book is dedicated to Ron Lippitt, my father and mentor. It is also dedicated to Ed Lindaman, co-developer of the Preferred Futuring process, who with Ron pioneered the way for the rest of us. Ron survived Ed by four years and deeply felt the loss of a beloved colleague. He went on to further develop Preferred Futuring and share it as widely as he could.

This book is the result of twenty-five years of work and countless futuring events. Writing it has been a continued partnership with Ron. Sometimes it was as if we were in conversation even as I held the pen. His wisdom and knowledge, as much as my own, are embedded in the words here.

Ron has been dead for twelve years. Many of us for whom he was a mentor and major influence have honored his work by carrying on as flame bearers, continuing to pioneer where he left off. I want to express my deep appreciation for the work of colleagues like Kathie Dannemiller, Marv Weisbord, Billie Alban, and Barbara Bunker for their contributions to the field of futuring and large system change.

I would like to thank the many participants over the past fifteen years of the Planned Change Internship with whom I have been able to share Preferred Futuring, who have carried it out and applied it in their work in organizations, and shared their excitement and stories afterward. I want to express my deep appreciation and admiration to the many leaders and leadership teams who have when necessary taken the risks to make the process work in their system and been committed to supporting the common dream and making it work. And most important, I thank them for their trust in me as well as in the process.

My very deep appreciation goes to Valerie Barth, who believed in this project enough to convince others that it was an important and worthy enterprise. It was she, with the help of Alis Valencia, Steve Piersanti, and others at Berrett-Koehler Publishers, who have midwifed this birthing.

I want to personally thank Robert Jacobs, Sandra Janoff, Dennis Reina, Gates McKibbin, and Kathryn Wall for their reviews of the manuscript and very helpful and specific feedback, which greatly improved this book. And very special thanks to Charlie Dorris, who labored patiently with me page by page to arrive at the book's final form and structure. And thanks also to Ellen Sharphorn, who helped in the typing of early draft materials, and to Judy Faye Carmichel, who developed many of the graphic models eventually used in this book.

I want to state my personal appreciation to Peggy Lippitt; thanks, mom, for your support. Most of all to Sylvia Carter, my dear wife and life partner, thank you for your understanding and support all the way. I love you more each day.

L.L.L.

May the collective energy and knowledge placed in this book
be of benefit to all human and other living systems.
Ohm Ah Hum.

P A R T 1

A Preview of Preferred Futuring

In Part One, the Introduction discusses the underlying philosophy of Preferred Futuring and some of its key concepts. Chapter One then provides a history of Preferred Futuring, and Chapter Two previews the eight steps in the Preferred Futuring process and illustrates how that process has been used.

Introduction

What Is Preferred Futuring?

As events have accelerated, particularly in these last thirty years or so, we have begun to realize that we really are able to create much of our own future—that there is a relationship between what we want and what we can do and create. That is the main point about thinking in future tense: a new recognition that we are able to construct a very large part of our own future.

The Birth of Preferred Futuring

In the late '50s and early '60s, Ron Lippitt—who was by training a social scientist—was searching for better ways to help groups set the right goals and to initiate change. He noticed that although the steps might vary, people used a basic problem-solving process. They usually listed all the current problems, applied a set of criteria to prioritize them, decided on a most important or root problem, developed action strategies and steps, implemented the plan, and evaluated it.

Ron began to research this conventional problem-solving process, using audiotape excerpts from a variety of groups involved in setting goals and developing plans. These involved executive teams, city planners, health care leaders, church boards, and many others over the next few years. As he listened in to the proceedings, he became shocked by what he found:

- As the list of problems was created for prioritization, and then discussed, the level of motivation and energy in the groups would

3

diminish. After thirty to forty-five minutes, there might be only one person or a minority subgroup exhorting the rest to continue the work.

- There was a constant rise in comments attributing the causes of the problems to factors outside the group and its sphere of control or influence.
- When groups were able to get to the point of goal setting, the goals were usually shortsighted and not very creative. (Today we would say they were not *breakthrough* goals.)
- The goals were generally an attempt to move away from something undesirable or even painful, and were not motivated by a desire to move toward something exciting.
- When problems were listed and prioritized, the resulting depression, sense of helplessness, and defensiveness often made it more difficult for work groups to cooperate or follow through with action. More infighting and blaming was produced.

Ron Lippitt compared these results with results from a new process that was to become Preferred Futuring. In this new process, the focus was not on problem solving but on listing what was working as well as not working, and then creating an exciting and collective vision of a desired future state. This was followed by generating action goals and action plans to implement that vision, and finally taking action and evaluating it. Ron Lippitt was very excited by what he found in the comparative research:

- When people were asked to list what *was* working as well as what was not working, it created an air of honesty and realism as well as a much-needed catharsis. There was a sense of dissatisfaction about a part of what was, not a sense of defeatism.
- When a picture of a preferred future was created, excitement and enthusiasm rose markedly. The sense of excitement and joy was a dramatic change from the depression and blaming of problem-solving groups.
- Goals were much more far-reaching and creative (what we would call *stretch* or *breakthrough* in nature).

- There was a definite air of increased motivation based on moving toward something exciting rather than moving away from something painful and to be avoided. There was an increased willingness to co-operate and work together as a team.
- The high level of energy and empowerment generated during the futuring phase seemed to carry groups well into the action-taking phase. It seemed like a way of splitting the human energy atom had been discovered.

Ron Lippitt is one of the founders of Preferred Futuring, and after he died in 1987, many of us carried on using the principles of Preferred Futuring and further developing them. Preferred Futuring has now been used with tens of thousands of groups and organizations. It has been added to and developed by many of us who have learned and incorporated Preferred Futuring into our practice as consultants, supervisors, managers, and leaders. This paradigm shift has moved us from focusing on the problem to focusing on an exciting future state. The basic steps involved in the two paradigms are different.

Problem Solving
- List problems
- Prioritize problems
- Determine strategic starting point
- Plan actions to solve problems

Preferred Futuring
- Review how we got here
- List what is working and not working
- Determine the future you want
- Plan actions to achieve preferred future

And the deliverables or results are different.

Problem Solving
- A list of problems
- Key problem identification
- A solution
- Action plans to achieve a solution

Preferred Futuring
- A sense of heritage
- A realistic assessment
- An exciting destination
- Success criteria
- Action plans to create future of choice

What has made Preferred Futuring so widely accepted?

Preferred Futuring:
Thinking in Terms of the Whole System

Many of you have heard the story about the couple who are sitting in one end of a rowboat, both very calm and enjoying the scenery. In the other end of the boat, another couple are furiously bailing water that is pouring in from a hole in the bottom of the boat. One member of the calm couple says to the other, "Aren't you glad that hole is in their end of the boat?" Today, more than at any time in history, and regardless of whether we are talking about a department or an entire organization or a community—any system—we understand that the hole is never in *their* end of the boat; it's always in *our boat*.

When people realize we are all connected because we are a part of the same system, people are thinking in terms of "whole systems." Because we are connected, we influence and are influenced by other parts of the system, whether we are aware of this or not. Any organization or community is bound by often unseen fabrics of interconnected actions. Whole-systems thinking requires that we realize we are part of that fabric and not exempt or removed. When we are part of a complex system, this connection is less obvious than it is in that rowboat example, but it is just the same.

Whole-systems thinking requires that we shift how we think and act. We must get involved, rather than taking the attitude that it is not our problem or the business of our department. We must realize that no department can be excellent unless the whole system is excellent. The popular analogy that makes this point is that you don't build a world-class car by roaming the world and assembling a world-class carburetor from one vehicle and then a world-class engine from another and then a world-class transmission from another until you have all the necessary parts. When you try to assemble them, they will not fit together. In like fashion a finance department can model itself after the best finance department in the world, but this may not make it a successful department in the system of which it is a part.

The Preferred Futuring process is a whole-systems way of thinking. It focuses on getting all stakeholders in the room to participate in deciding upon and creating the future they feel passionate about. People listen to others in order to see the world and the system as others see it. These different views are integrated and the apparent chaos rationalized by noticing underlying structures or patterns that give new and deeper understanding, an understanding that can lead to insight and innovation.

Preferred Futuring and whole-systems thinking mean resisting the urge for the quick fix. They mean staying open to inquiry and suspending judgment—being open to having our truth (how we see the world) changed or broadened. And it may mean realizing that giving up some efficiency in our department (some sacrifice on our part) is best for the whole system and is making a choice that supports the whole system.

In addition to Preferred Futuring helping us think in terms of the whole, it also helps us think in the future tense, something that is critically important in our rapidly changing world. Ed Lindaman, a cofounder of Preferred Futuring, used to talk about the importance of a future tense orientation. I've tried to capture those thoughts in the next section.

The Philosophy of Preferred Futuring

Each of us needs to learn how to think in the future tense for himself or herself.[1] In other words, what is important is not predictions of the future, but crystallizing in our own mind what our own preferred future is. What is our vision of what we want?

In 1974 and 1975, when Ed Lindaman chaired the governor's change task force on the future of the state of Washington—a program involving sixty thousand people and representing the three million people in the entire state—people like Alvin Toffler called it the most sophisticated citizen participation program in the history of the world.[2]

Ed discovered that it was a very exciting experience, asking anybody—a farmer, a teacher, a homemaker, a mechanic, a teenager—for their images of a preferred future. In seminars, in small groups, on call-in television, and in many other ways, Ed's team asked, "What is it you want for the future of the state of Washington?" At first they'd say, "My word, nobody's ever asked me that before. You mean you really want to know?" Ed's team would reply, "Yes, we really want to know." Then these citizens would pour out beautiful images about what they wanted for their future.

Ed's thesis: If you can find a way to ask people their vision about a doable future, and then listen to them and put it down, a creative image of a preferred future can begin to take shape.

In the past, people tended to assume the future was going to repeat the present. As events have accelerated, particularly these last thirty years or so, we have begun to realize that we really are able to create much of our own future—that there is a relationship between what we want and what we can do and create. That is the main point about thinking in future tense: a new recognition that we are able to construct a very large part of our own future. This was point one of Ed's thesis.

This leads to point two: If we accept that we are able to construct our own future, then we have to decide if we want to actively involve ourselves in that future. Or do we want to get a can of beer and a TV and just sit there and let others decide our future for us? We have to decide whether to intentionally involve ourselves in that exciting and creative act of choosing and implementing preferred futures.

This leads to point three: Once we decide to get involved, we have to decide *how* to participate in the creation of our own future or the future of our society or company or city or state.

Point four is critical: We have to decide what kind of future we prefer. This gets us down to the tough questions about what we really value and what we really want. We have to begin to make choices, knowing that predicting the future isn't enough. We have to know what our intentions are. Many of us haven't been taught to think that way. We have to learn to think in the future tense. Otherwise we will be manipulated by people and things around us as if we were robots.

Toffler, in his book *Learning for Tomorrow,* has a very useful illustration that helps us understand this point.[3] He talks in that book about a tribe of natives in a remote rain forest. It is a primitive tribe disconnected from the rest of civilization. This tribe has always lived on the river. Its people derive their livelihood from the river. Their world is fifty miles around, and they have been there for centuries, and so when a child is born in that culture, the parents think right away, "How do we prepare this child to live in the future that will be?"

They would not say it just this way, but they want to educate this child to survive. So on what do they base that? They say, "We've always lived on this river, our ancestors lived on this river according to our legends, so obviously life will be with the river. We have to teach each child whatever it takes to live on a river." So they prepare this child to live in the future, based upon what has happened and what is happening. That seems very legitimate and logical.

This is exactly what we tend to do today in our own culture. We prepare young people to live in the future based on what has been and what is.

To continue the story, unknown to this tribe, another tribe lives a hundred miles upriver. They have developed technology capable of building dams. They are spending their days building a dam on this river. In six months there will not be any water down below for the first tribe.

That symbolizes some of the problem that rapidly changing technology is creating for most of us. To live in the future, not only do we have to prepare ourselves based on what has been and what is, we have to educate ourselves for the future. And that education must be based not only on what has happened and what is happening but also on what we think will happen.

The Freedom to Choose a Better Future

Freedom—we all want it. We all try to create conditions and do things to be free. But freedom also means being able to actively and consciously participate in the creation of our own future. If your future is decided by others, you really are not free. So there is a relationship between freedom and our willingness to determine what our future will be.

How then can we decide best about our own future? We make the best decisions when we are in community with others of a shared interest. Freedom is related to our ability to come together as a community and create a collective preferred future. We need a place where we can talk back and forth about what it is we prefer. Where we can change and analyze it and reflect upon it. Where we don't have to sell ourselves. Our ability to project a collective preferred future ultimately defines our community and empowers us as a community.

The nature of any future horizon that we hold—what we prefer—is such that as we move toward it, it changes. This is natural. Anyone who has an image of a future that is unchangeable is going to be in trouble. Conditions will change and each of us will change. There is always a dynamic relationship between each of us and the image of the preferred future we envision. Each of us must remember and know that anyone developing an image of a preferred future need not worry about it being permanent. Even though you may enjoy what you are doing, if life went on and on as it is now, you would become much less excited about your future.

Deep within each of us is a desire, a hope, for a better future. It is engraved deep in our souls. Whether we can articulate it clearly or not, there is a desire for something better, something closer to our preferred future. It is hope that moves us into the future. We carry time around in our heads as memory and hope. If we do not go far enough back in our memories or far enough forward in our hopes, the present is impoverished.

Everything that is possible now was at one time impossible. When we look forward with hope and expectation, it is an act of creating that empowers and creates the present we want. So we must learn to speak out and say, "yes, this is where we prefer to go." This is the future that people working together want. It is the future that makes possible what we do in the present.

Let's say you decide to search out the future. What happens? You step over boundaries of the present into the future. Now imagine yourself five years into the future. What do you prefer for your life? You may begin by musing over an infinite array of possibilities. Suppose you decide to sail around the world with your spouse and drop anchor in Tahiti and scuba dive and live it up for two years.

As you contemplate those next two years, something very magical happens. You are immediately transported back to the present. You are now forced to contemplate the impact of your present actions on that preferred future. You had better learn radio communication and meteorology. You will have to be able to captain a boat. You will have to learn geography to find all those beautiful inlets.

Immediately, future hope and expectation begin to transform your present. The future is always now! The bottom line is that if you do not have an idea of your preferred future for yourself, for your organization, for your city, for your job, or whatever, you are very limited and not free. Thinking in the future tense from a perspective of clarity about what you want becomes an act of creation in the present.

Let's look at this another way. Pretend that when you get up tomorrow morning the next twenty-four hours will be a microcosm of your future. You hold certain assumptions and beliefs about the future for those twenty-four hours. These assumptions will allow you to move through this time period with clarity and rationality. In fact, without them you would have a horrible time. What are those assumptions you have about your life, job, place of work? Will these also work for the next five years?

Creation is not over. It is barely under way. In ten thousand years we may be colonizing planets all over the galaxy. Twenty-fifth-century people will look back at the twentieth-century primitives. There is more to come. The exciting and beautiful thing about it is we have been given an opportunity to consciously participate. Hopes and intentions are acts of creation that Preferred Futuring helps us move toward.

It remains to be seen how each of us will respond to the future. But there are three possible responses.

First, we can try to resist it. We all know people who try to resist or block the future. And we all need to acknowledge that tendency in ourselves.

Second, we can adapt. When Ed Lindaman lived in Los Angeles and was trying to adapt to the smog and traffic, he used to say, "If I ever get mad enough, I will get myself a gas mask." But he realized that was ridiculous. There are some things to which you don't want to adapt.

Third, we can invent. We can consciously create our own and our collective future of choice. What is it? Who will shape it?

Back in 1971, in his famous book *The Future of the Future,* John McHale said something like this: "The question is no longer can we change the world? The question is what kind of world do we want?"[4] That encapsulates all of what this book is about. We are beginning now to really assess the ultimate human impact of change. We must begin now to decide what it is we want.

Preferred Futuring Today

This book makes available the Preferred Futuring concept developed by Ron Lippitt and Ed Lindaman in 1968, and subsequently enhanced by others, including the author of this book. Preferred Futuring is a progenitor for many of the large-scale methodologies in use today, such as Kathie Dannemiller's Large Scale Change methodology and Marv Weisbord's Future Search methodology, and for the work of many other consultants, leaders, and managers. But as I will show in this book, Preferred Futuring retains a distinctive characteristic: the flexibility with which it can be used is unmatched.

Preferred Futuring is suitable for any kind and any size organization. It can be used at a single event attended by all stakeholders, or in a series of events. Stakeholders outside the organization can be integrated into the process in a variety of ways. And not least (and the purpose of this book), Preferred Futuring does not require an outside consultant or other third party. After reading this book, you will be able to use Preferred Futuring in your department, organization, community—in whatever system you find yourself.

Preferred Futuring is the most powerful, robust, and adaptable tool that we have available today to bring order out of chaos and to create the results we want. If a group of people use Preferred Futuring to connect with their passions and focus on the same thing that they all want, this will most likely produce the desired result.

I do not make this claim lightly. After thirty years of using Preferred Futuring, we now know much more about the phenomenon, its dynamics and creative power, and why it works when it is done right and used appropriately. As this book will demonstrate, "doing it right" means creating a specific future reality from the point of view of an entire organization or community or group of people who are connected—what I call a whole system. "Using it appropriately" means mobilizing the collective energy and creativity and passion of that whole system, not just of a few of its members.

The basic paradigm shift of focusing on the future we want rather than on the problems we face has been profound and far-reaching and has rippled around the world. The process of Preferred Futuring offers a way to make that paradigm shift and to operate out of our passion rather than out of our fears. This book, for the first time, tells the story, presents the model, summarizes the steps, shares key learnings, and offers many applications and practical tools that allow you to use Preferred Futuring for yourself.

1

The History of
Preferred Futuring

Each of us needs to learn how to think in the future tense, to crystallize our vision of what we want. The question is no longer can I change the world, but what kind of world do I want?

The Paradigm Shift

Preferred Futuring represents a paradigm shift from the traditional problem-solving methods for creating change. Our orientation moves from focusing on a problem and fixing it to focusing on exactly what future situation we want and taking action to get there. Research and experience have shown how Preferred Futuring stimulates creativity, innovation, and motivation for action.

Preferred Futuring can align a group of individuals with a common direction, generate widespread support, put targets for improvement in focus, and link vision to action, while having a definite team-building or community-building effect. It allows any team, company, or community to collectively create tangible pathways to the future it wants. It has been successfully used to promote civic interests and general welfare in communities and regional areas and to develop programs at these levels to enhance quality of life for citizens. It has also been used to provide a strategic focus for a total organization and its leadership or to encourage development of divisional and departmental goals and activities. Preferred Futuring has consistently resulted in greater use of resources aligned and focused as a total system, enhanced product or service quality and productivity, increased cost-effectiveness and work satisfaction, and more purposeful movement to a culture of teamwork and cooperation.

A brief history of Preferred Futuring will give you a deeper understanding of this concept.

Reviewing the History of Preferred Futuring

As the United States emerged from the Second World War, we faced great social and technological change. Television, nuclear energy, and many other technological advances were about to change our lives for better or worse. There was at this time a small band of behavioral scientists, composed of Dr. Kurt Lewin and his protégés, one of whom was Dr. Ronald Lippitt. They were deeply committed to democratic philosophy and principles. Lewin had been profoundly influenced by his experience as a Jew who fled Nazi Germany. He was convinced that small face-to-face groups were the way to combat anti-Semitism, and through his research, he became the "grandfather" of Group Dynamics theory and practices.

In the Second World War, Ron Lippitt had been in the Navy and during that time had worked with Margaret Mead and other behavioral scientists. As a result of his work, commando teams used a more participative leadership style and achieved a much higher level of performance.

Ron developed two passions that were to drive him all his professional life. The first was a commitment to the use of social science knowledge. He was adamant about putting scientific knowledge in the hands of the practitioner and not having it filter into the marketplace ten years later from scientific journals. His second passion was to expose the impact of autocratic leadership on human systems. His doctoral research did just that. His research into the impact of authoritarian, democratic, and laissez-faire leadership styles on human performance and systems still stands today as a basis for much of the later work on leadership theories and models.[1]

The Early Years

In the 1940s, these social scientists clearly saw the need for planning rather than letting drift be the steering mechanism for the years ahead. This implied, for them, the need to train leaders to plan using procedures that involved people in participative ways, if the planning was going to work. They quickly learned that nonleadership personnel in systems also needed training in the skills of participation. Their efforts to implement participative leadership were the driving force behind what happened for the next fifty years.

This small band of social scientists found themselves at MIT. Support was hard to find. As Ron once put it, they were housed in the basement of a building so ancient that when someone flushed a toilet you could hear it travel right over your head in the open pipes below the ceiling. Yet their lives were about to be changed. At the University of Michigan, Kenneth Kenniston was the very liberal dean (referred to by some as the "red" dean) of Graduate Studies. He saw Group Dynamics as a future force and made Lewin, Lippitt, and the others in the research team an offer they didn't refuse. This group was to participate in the birth of the Institute for Social Research a few years later.

Kurt Lewin's early death in 1947 was a blow to Ron and his colleagues. Carrying on his legacy, they went on to become the founders of what has come to be called the Group Dynamics movement. This became a very powerful and transformative methodology for opening up honest dialogue about needs people have and how to mobilize creative, innovative, and collective action with each other.

Applying Change Theory to Larger Groups

In the 1950s Ron began to apply the rapidly growing knowledge about small groups to larger systems. He coined the term "planned change" in the seminal work *The Dynamics of Planned Change*, which he wrote with Watson and Westley (1958).[2] That change could be planned and that we could be proactive caused a basic shift in thinking for many. Other valuable findings were that all change processes in any size human system evidenced predictable dynamics and that change in human systems had three stages—unfreezing, changing, and refreezing. The concept of "change agents" was developed.

This all led to the application of knowledge about change to larger intergroup systems known as organizations and communities. Thus, in the 1960s, this became the knowledge and skill base called "organization development" and stimulated larger systems change methodologies. The concept of change agent evolved into the role of organization development consultant.

The Perception of Change Changes

In the 1960s Ron began to see that the nature of change was quite different from what we had believed it to be. This was a radical notion at the time, but is readily accepted today. Ron Lippitt posited that:

Change *Was*	Change *Is Now*
Orderly	Chaotic
Logical	Organic
Controllable	Uncontrollable
Incremental	Continuous

This new perception rendered the old three-phase model of change—unfreezing, changing, and refreezing—less useful. Change, in fact, seemed to be a continuous and unpredictable phenomenon. The only predictable thing about change was its certainty and necessity for any living system. The absence of change meant death or entropy of a system. The days of refreezing and having smooth sailing for a while were coming to an end. And systems were becoming more complex. Further insights were now needed into why planned change efforts worked or didn't work.

In the late 1960s Ron began searching for new ways to look at change and better ways to be an agent of positive change. It was at this time that he became acquainted with futurist Ed Lindaman. In the early 1970s, as director of program planning for the design and manufacture of the Apollo Space Craft with Rockwell International's Space Division, Ed mobilized the whole organization with the single focused vision of placing a man on the moon for that first step. This was a key factor in how they accomplished this very complex and difficult task. Ron became deeply influenced by Ed and the field of futuring. For

Ron, managing change was in fact about creating the future. It fit! First he noticed, from his experience in the field of change management, that there were four basic human responses to change in any human system:

- *Holding on to the past.* This often looked like resistance to change. There would be comments like, "Why fix it if it isn't broken?" or "Let's go back to the way we used to do it. That always worked."
- *Focusing on and responding to the pain or the problem.* This was the most typical response, and it often included a set of problem-solving steps. The hope was that a solution to the problem or reduction of the pain would be achieved.
- *Attempts to* predict *the future.* This was epitomized by one of the two schools of futuring that focused on trend data gathering and analysis. The strategy was to gather the right kind of trend data, analyze the information correctly, be standing in the right place at the right time when the future arrived, and cash in. This has proved to be defective in many cases. For example, it was predicted a long time ago that we would run out of food on the planet. But on the way to the future we created new grains that are much more prolific and resistant to disease, thus upsetting these predictions.
- *Preferred Futuring.* This was epitomized by the other school of futuring, which focused on developing possible scenarios and selecting the future of choice. Action plans and steps could then be made to create the future of choice. Ed Lindaman was a proponent of this school.

Ed Lindaman helped Ron Lippitt and the rest of us begin to "think in the future tense." People were helped to prioritize desired future possibilities, scan for environmental trends, and think and act more proactively and less reactively as groups and organizations to create a future they wanted to see. Preferred Futuring concepts and methods had worked to get a man to the moon and back safely, and now they began working to help other organizations and communities manage complex challenges to achieve their preferred future.

Preferred Futuring Comes of Age

During the late 1960s Lippitt and Lindaman shared their experiences and clarified the contrast between choosing the future you prefer as opposed to trying to predict it or taking a traditional problem-solving approach in organizations. They coined the term *Preferred Futuring.* As discussed in the Introduction, Ron conducted research comparing typical problem solving approaches and this new Preferred Futuring approach as a way to mobilize and focus action for planned change.

In 1970 Lindaman and Lippitt collaborated as members of a long-range planning task force of the National Council of the YMCA. The Preferred Futuring methodology was clarified and implemented in a series of projects and workshops and later in a week-long Futuring and Planning workshop at the National Training Laboratories. The two ended up collaborating on the first and only jointly authored publication, a booklet titled *Choosing the Future You Prefer,* in 1979.[3]

Ed Lindaman and Ron Lippitt gave us a basic and important new way to look at change. The shift was from problem solving to Preferred Futuring. In 1981 Lindaman died suddenly of a rare infection during a trip to China. Ron deeply felt Ed Lindaman's loss but continued to further develop and evolve the Preferred Futuring approach, involving many people, organizations, and communities. During the period from 1981 through 1985, Ron conducted over eighty Preferred Futuring workshops and events in communities and organizations. Preferred Futuring provided a solution for leaders and managers who were looking for ways to involve people more widely in planning, link planning to action, improve effectiveness of developing breakthrough solutions, or focus the whole team or larger organization in a strategic direction.

Conclusion

When Ron died in 1987, many of us carried on, using the principles of Preferred Futuring and further developing them. How Preferred Futuring is practiced today—the eight steps of the Preferred Futuring process—are previewed in Chapter Two.

2

The Basic Steps
in Preferred Futuring

Deep within each of us is a desire, a hope for a better future. It is engraved on our souls. If you find a way to ask people, listen, and write it down, an image of that future can begin to take shape.

Previewing the Process

Part Two of this book explains in depth the Preferred Futuring process, but to put each step into some perspective, this chapter will preview all the steps and provide several examples of how Preferred Futuring has been used.

The Preferred Futuring Process consists of eight steps:

1. History
2. Current State
3. Core Values and Beliefs
4. Events, Trends, and Developments
5. Preferred Future Vision
6. Action Goals
7. Plan and Rehearse
8. Implement and Follow Up

I do not mean to imply that Preferred Futuring is a linear process. As shown in Figure 2.1, the Preferred Futuring Model allows organizations and systems to recycle through the process, which as I will discuss, is the best way to use it.

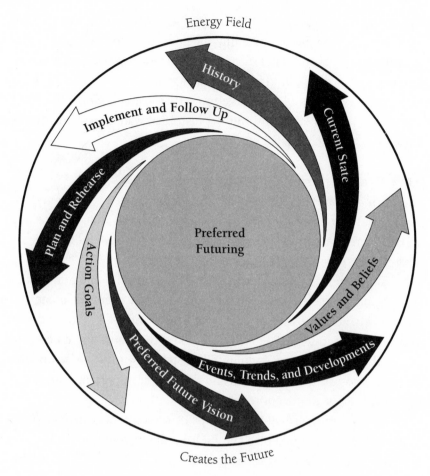

Energy Field

Steps to generate the energy field that manifests the future you want

Figure 2.1   The Preferred Futuring Model

Step One: Review History

The Historical Review creates a shared sense and appreciation of the organization's common history.

This step may consist of interviewing several old-timers, panel style, about the way things used to be, the significant events that shaped the organization, and some of the good and bad times. Or a large time line graphic with some key events and dates can be created before the meeting; the graphic is on the wall when people arrive, and they are asked before the meeting officially starts to place on it other significant events and dates, using Post-it notes. Then the graphic can be reviewed at the desired place on the agenda.

This review should not take more than thirty to forty-five minutes. It is merely a fast skim over the historical waters to clarify briefly how we got here and what our roots are.

Step Two: Identify What's Working and What's Not

Identifying what Ron called *Prouds* and *Sorries* creates a common database about our current situation. Prouds are things that are working in the current situation, about which we are proud, and Sorries are things that are not working, about which we are sorry.

This step is usually done in table groups, even if five hundred or a thousand people are involved simultaneously or over time in smaller sessions. Table groups are asked to brainstorm and list Prouds and Sorries for a few minutes. Then they are asked to discuss these items, to clarify their thoughts and feelings. Ultimately they must come up with the three most important Prouds and three most important Sorries and report those out to the entire group.

An hour in the small table groups before reports is often enough. The reports are recorded on a central list and the common database of proudest Prouds and sorriest Sorries is acknowledged. This is an important time of honest sharing and catharsis.

Step Three: Identify Values and Beliefs

This step clarifies the underlying values and beliefs that have determined the organization's actions, and also the values and beliefs that we also want to influence us in the future.

The table groups can be asked to identify and discuss underlying values and beliefs that exist and report these out for general discussion. Candor is important; groups need to call out beliefs such as "All is hopeless" or "Leadership will do what they want anyway" if that's what people believe, as well as positive beliefs such as "We are in a situation of tremendous opportunity" and so on. It is also important to call out values such as "customer focus," "people are important," "stockholders are more important than workers," and so on. Participants discuss which values and beliefs to keep or leave behind. This can lead to establishing new guiding principles or reconnecting with the useful old ones.

This step may take as much time as the previous one. But it is important to move the process along and not get bogged down here.

Step Four: Identify Relevant Events, Developments, and Trends

Analyzing the events, developments, and trends that may have an impact on us as we move to our preferred future allows us to proactively plan better.

People are asked to brainstorm and list the things they see coming over the horizon or developing now that will affect them as they move toward the future they want. These might include developments in technology, marketplace changes, legislative or regulatory changes, recent company policy decisions, and so on. This can be a thirty- to forty-five-minute listing and sharing activity at tables with some discussion of how these will affect us in a positive or negative way.

At this juncture, it is also possible to bring in customers and ask them what their future needs will be or to bring in some expert to share the events, trends, and developments in various areas strategic to the organization.

Step Five: Create a Preferred Future Vision

A Preferred Future Vision is clear, detailed, and commonly understood; this vision consists of a set of specific images, a set of strategic priorities. All participants (or at least a critical mass) are aligned to the vision, feel a sense of investment or ownership in it, and clearly understand their role.

People are asked to create a specific description of the future, two to five years from now, that really pleases them. They describe what they see that indicates the change effort has been totally successful. They write down what they see, what people are saying in the halls, what the customers are saying, what the media are saying and so on. This is done as part of a journey into the future, and the description is written in the present tense—what they actually see and hear and read as they visit the future they want.

After they do this alone, they share their descriptions at tables and create a master list. Table groups then post their preferred future images and read all the others. Votes are cast by all and priorities are established. The results are reviewed, discussed, and agreed upon as the strategic priorities—the images that constitute the Preferred Vision. This produces a vision statement that could be twenty pages long with five to ten strategic priorities, under which is included detailed information that describes success. This "Preferred Future Vision" document is not the one-sentence or one-paragraph "vision statement" often referred to these days.

By this time the amount of breakthrough thinking and creativity surprises most of the participants. Excitement and motivation run high. Many feel a new optimism. Only a few may still remain skeptical.

Step Six: Translate Future Visions into Action Goals

Teams are formed around each of the five to ten Preferred Future images identified in the prior step. They clarify each image by creating a more detailed description of what that future looks like, and then they translate that into several action goals. Some goals may be intermediate and some may be two-year goals. These are then shared with all other teams, who listen and add ideas to be considered.

The key task in this step is to put legs on the vision, to link vision to action.

Step Seven: Plan for Action

The Action Plan will consist of specific planned steps with accountabilities identified.

For each of the Action Goals created in the prior step, planning teams are established that develop action plans that include who, what, how, and when. It is important to build in milestones and ways to celebrate reaching these milestones as part of the action commitments.

Assigning responsibility for follow-through must also be part of these plans.

Step Eight: Create a Structure
for Implementing the Plan

For the implementation to succeed, monitoring and support functions must be ongoing. Data about the progress of the change effort must be collected, analyzed, and used to make midcourse corrections if necessary. Celebrations and successes need to be publicized and made part of the new mythology and stories of the system.

In addition, Preferred Futuring must be a continuous and cyclical process, not a one-time event or series of events that ends with taking action. The vision should drive the yearly business goals. Updating the vision can be made part of the yearly business planning cycle and process.

Specific Application Examples

The eight steps in the Preferred Futuring process are simple and adaptable to any context: public, private, or civic, large or small, national or international, face-to-face or virtual, a product focus or a service focus. They must, however, be initiated within some context, for example, to create a strategic direction and plan for company alignment with a specific picture of success, or to develop a concrete plan for a project team that is supported by all members, or to establish a strategic alliance between two systems. The steps take on a life of their own when applied to specific situations, such as those discussed in this section.

Grassroots Constituencies in Statewide Strategic Planning

The board of an agency that delivered services to all developmentally disabled citizens in its state requested help to involve constituents in a strategic planning process. The board set up a planning team representing service deliverers, recipients, administrators, and the consultants.

The result was a series of four regional events. On the first day of each regional event, a board panel heard testimony from local people who received and gave service, testimony regarding the effectiveness and state of services. This was done in a town-meeting-like atmosphere. The second day was a Preferred Futuring event. The prior day's testimony information was reviewed, and table groups consisting of the same people who had given the testimony developed a vision of the future that would be innovative, reduce current shortcomings, and meet constituent needs. This was done at small tables and then shared across the whole room of several hundred people. Priorities were then determined. This was replicated in all four regions of the state within a month.

As the regional futuring sessions generated data, it was combined with all other regional results. The collective priorities were determined and regional representatives were solicited to participate in the final two-day plenary event. The purpose was to report the results and develop specific action priorities and recommendations that would become the statewide strategic plan.

The plan was written based on the vision of the future desired by the stakeholders in the system. The board was very glad to have a clear mandate on which to base requests of the state legislature. The strategic planning people were ecstatic knowing their efforts were based on well-documented stakeholder data and widespread support for follow-through.

Eliminating a Bottleneck

In the engine division of a Big Three automotive company in the United States, the engine pricing process was a bottleneck, holding up production for all the product platforms. As part of the typical data gathering to determine what the current process really was, we also asked stakeholders, including internal customers, what the new process would look like if it were working to their needs. They described how people were acting, what was being said in high-level management meetings, and what ultimate customers were saying a year later that really pleased them and indicated that the process improvement project was a total success.

A cross-functional team then analyzed these data and identified the current process. Then the Preferred Future data were used to describe what the improved process would look like, based on what stakeholders had said. The results of this were used to create an innovative process and a highly successful implementation effort. The Preferred Future process added richness, depth, and creativity to the results. It also provided important success criteria. The Preferred Futuring process helped people to detach from their own turf enough to come up with a new pricing process and plan that really met the needs of customers and other stakeholders.

Moving Beyond Conflict in a Voluntary Organization

An ecumenical campus ministry of a major Midwestern university was in turmoil. Because its sources of funding were declining and the mix of the student body was changing, the ministry needed to choose which services to offer and whether to continue traditional services or offer outreach programs. The board president and the co-directors of the staff were badly split over the future direction of this hundred-year-old organization.

The staff and board attended a strategic planning retreat. The historical review began as people entered. On the wall was a time line chart that included historical pictures and milestones of the organization. As participants arrived, they updated the time line with their personal input about significant developments in the life of this organization.

During the meeting, people would refer back to the time line and tell stories about student advocacy and support of student social action organizations, describing the significant impacts on people's lives these had. It was a powerful experience and all participants recognized that this organization had provided major nurturing to the founding and development of two of the most powerful student social action organizations of the '60s. This provided a more positive context in which to list Prouds (what was working now) and Sorries (what was not working now). Identifying and analyzing the current and future events, developments, and trends provided further data that people could agree upon.

Then individuals were asked to develop a preferred picture of what the organization would look like in two years, including what students were saying about the organization, what the media were saying, and how the board and staff were working together and what activities were taking place that really pleased them. These visions were shared at tables. This allowed the start of dialogue between the clearly divided factions. Tables created a composite list and the total group decided on priorities from all these lists via a nominating process.

The dialogue with regard to differences was much more focused and productive in the context of a desired future. Agreement on strategic priorities was reached, as long-standing conflicts were aired and dealt with successfully. The board and staff were able to move forward with excitement and a sense of teamwork.

In the process, the board president discovered that her own priorities were not in line with those of the larger organization. Later, she was able to resign in a very positive way, without the bitterness that sometimes attends such separations.

Turning a City Around

A medium-sized city in the upper Midwest had seen steady economic and population decline for a number of years. Many were becoming alarmed. A small group of concerned citizens became excited about using Preferred Futuring to return hope and a proactive spirit to people and save the city from its downward spiral.

The first step was to mobilize grassroots leaders and respected members of the community, whether they were business people, clergy, retiree volunteers, or whatever. These people were nominated by the initial group of concerned citizens and invited to a meeting where they were introduced to the Preferred Futuring process and asked to join the proposed project. This led to a funded program with a project office and volunteers.

Volunteers were trained in Preferred Futuring, and they convened futuring sessions in school cafeterias, church halls, and civic meeting areas. The local papers publicized and covered the events lavishly. Over a nine-month period most children and adults had been part of developing a picture of their community in the future, a picture that excited them. These data were summarized and revealed at a citywide plenary session. Voluntary action groups who would implement the plan were provided with training and support. Resources and energy began to flow with focus to projects ranging from economic development to parks and recreational facilities.

In two years the city had attracted the new business it desired, improved its public areas, and had tremendous civic involvement. The newspapers had chronicled the events. A videotape was made of the success story. The president of the United States bestowed the City of the Year award, based on the dramatic turnaround and citizen involvement.

Integrating an Overwhelming Number of Priorities

Within a very large worldwide manufacturing organization, a product team was designing and developing an essential component for other business units. It was beset with an overwhelming number of "initiatives" dictated by the corporate leadership. The leadership and staff were highly competent, yet the stress of responding to initiatives each month in addition to getting their product out was rapidly raising the stress level and threatening to reduce productivity. Leadership was increasingly concerned that previously high morale and optimism was being seriously eroded.

A Preferred Futuring meeting was planned. Before the meeting, the leadership team met and members shared their honest feelings and thoughts about the increasingly impossible situation and their concern for the stress on the rest of the organization. This helped them to determine core priorities for the next three years.

The Preferred Futuring session began with an interview of the leadership team about the decisions and events that had led to the current situation, where everyone felt "my plate is too full for anything more." Others who had been in the organization for several years added their perspectives. This created a picture of how and why the intensity of demands and growing number of corporate initiatives had grown. The Prouds and Sorries activity uncovered some pride in accomplishing the impossible, anger at unrealistic demands that hampered effectiveness, and concerns that they couldn't keep it up. And when they checked in on their core operating values, they discovered that the stress had made sticking to them harder. This sounded an alarm and strengthened their resolve, because these values were important and had worked.

Then they painted an image of what the situation would look like after delivering their product on time by building on their current capabilities and turning corporate initiatives into sources of support for their goals. The result: They completely shifted from being overwhelmed and resentful to having a renewed sense of common vision and excitement.

This product team used an annual check-in event to see how they were doing and to revise the vision and action plans, and how they had "achieved the impossible" in three years. During this time and as the leadership began to apply itself to the next business cycle and its challenges, we periodically coached the leadership to recognize and celebrate the small wins along the way and the apparently impossible goals that the group had achieved.

Conclusion

The following chapters describe each step in more detail and include more specific how-to information, such as sample designs, worksheets, specific instructions for each step, and the tips and traps that we have learned. This material is designed to help you implement Preferred Futuring.

While these tools are here to save you time and avoid needlessly reinventing some things, please approach the tools with an eye to modifying them for your specific situation and not as the final word on the subject. They have all been used in specific situations and probably all have evolved from some earlier experience or idea. This is the nuts and bolts of how to do Preferred Futuring for whole-systems change, and the process is still evolving.

The Eight-Step Preferred Futuring Model

Part Two devotes one chapter to each of the eight steps in the Preferred Futuring Model. Think of these steps, and the tools that help you perform them, as pieces of an Erector set that can be used in a wide variety of ways, as will be shown in Part Three.

STEP 1: Review History

We carry time around in our heads as memory and hope. If we do not go far enough back in our memories or far enough forward in our hopes, the present is impoverished.

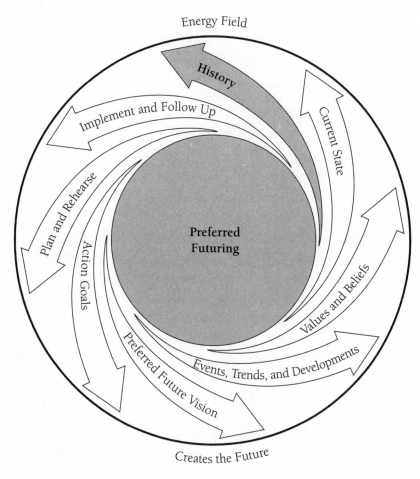

Steps to generate the energy field that manifests the future you want

Figure 3.1   History

Why Bother About the Past?

If we don't realize the importance of grounding ourselves in our past, it is very tempting to launch right into the more glamorous and exciting future vision step. Lewis Mumford observed that each period of history has its unique dominant themes and emergent themes.[1] As a civilization we have moved from hunting and other food gathering to agriculture, to industrialization, to information technology. This sort of reflection can give us a sense of movement through history. The dominant themes are easier to see, emergent themes more difficult. Reviewing our past can help make the emergent themes more visible and help us choose the future we want.

 TIP #1: Always connect with the past first, before imaging the future.

In his book *Transitions: Making Sense of Life's Changes,* William Bridges points out that we first have to let go before we can move on.[2] Elizabeth Kubler-Ross has made us all aware of the ending or mourning process necessary before we move on to what is next.[3] This is very powerful wisdom and we often fall into the trap of failing to heed it. To create and embrace an exciting future, we must acknowledge the good times and the bad, what must be kept and let go of. To do this, we must in turn acknowledge our roots. This helps us become aware of our biases and assumptions—biases and assumptions that may give us strength to move into the future or limit our ability to create that future. Remember the key purpose here: to learn from our past so that we can move on to our Preferred Future.

Examples of Reviewing History and Learning From It

The Historical Review has two phases: gathering data about our history, and drawing lessons and consequences from that historical data. This process allows us to gain a historical perspective with which to proceed through the remainder of the Preferred Futuring model.

The first two examples illustrate the first phase, and the third example illustrates both phases.

Scrolling Through History

Gathered for a three-day Preferred Futuring event are two hundred participants representing four levels of a statewide service organization with locations throughout the state. Faced with pending economic hardships, state and federal policy changes, and changing customer needs, they want to rapidly move the whole system to a team-based leadership culture, further decentralize their work processes, and reduce the cost of their operations.

As they enter the room, they find a long three-foot-high scroll on the wall. It is a time line in decades, starting with the birth of the organization and running up to the present. The instruction sheet they are handed asks them to enter their name at the point they joined the organization and to jot down on the scroll significant events in the life of the organization, especially those that contributed to its being where it is today. Categories of information are suggested, such as memories about economic or financial facts, names of leaders, significant decisions, achievements, or failures, and values or ethics that guided the organization in the past.

Early in the meeting, the time line is reviewed, and table groups are asked to decide on events that had positive or negative impact on the organization and contributed to its being where it is today. Representatives from each table group (runners) place red or blue dots on the three most positive or negative events. The results are reviewed, and this creates the basis for next exploring Prouds and Sorries and then the organization's norms, values, and guiding principles as the participants go further into the Preferred Future process.

Our Days on the Slope

At a Preferred Futuring event for the materials management division in a worldwide oil company, which focuses on moving forward after downsizing, over 150 participants begin reviewing history with several of the oldest members of the company's Alaska operation. These old-timers recall the early days up on "the Slope" where they had to cope with problems like fuel solidifying in the oil drums. The stories they tell give some of the newer employees a deeper sense of the history they are connected to and a broader perspective on current problems.

Learning from History

After interviewing the old-timers of a hospital staff, the entire group (which consists of three levels of the organization) is asked to probe such questions as, What can we learn from this past? How have we successfully coped with change before? How have we been inventive when faced with survival issues in the past? How have we opened up to new markets, techniques, or models in the past? What helped us innovate in the past? Is there anything we can learn about the need to take a longer-range view? As we summarize our learnings from our past, what does this tell us about how to act for the future?

The participants begin to realize that they have some past experience and resources to draw upon for help in meeting the new challenges they face. It helps create some optimism in the face of anticipated impending doom.

Tools for Gathering Data

Gathering Data, the first phase of the Historical Review, can be done using any one of the following tools:

- Decade call out
- Historical interview
- Time line start-up
- Review of past documentation

At the end of each of these activities, the group would go to the second phase of Historical Review: scanning the historical data for lessons and consequences; the tools for this second phase are discussed later in this chapter.

Decade Call Out

The Decade Call Out makes a broad-brush pass at the company's or institution's or group's past to find out what kinds of themes seemed to characterize (dominate) each decade. The result: A common sense of history, of how the organization has grown and developed over the years, and of where it has come from. This historical perspective gives clues to dealing with the future and fosters a readiness to look at where the organization is now.

Compared to the other historical review tools, the advantage of the Decade Call Out is that it requires no preparation, but can be done on the spot at the Preferred Futuring event.

The Decade Call Out is a three-step procedure:

1. With the entire group, set the stage by saying something like, "We want to take a walk through some of our history. This will help us shortly as we move into the future. We want you to list words (adjectives, nouns, phrases, slogans) that describe where we have been. We will do this in ten-year segments. Looking back at life here in our company [or institution, group, or whatever] during the period of 1950 to 1960 [for example] who was here then? What words can you think of that describe that time period? [List on a flip chart or an overhead if it is a large group.] How about 1960 to 1970?" Move forward through the relevant decades. Here are some categories to stimulate ideas:

*   Milestones in development and growth
*   Achievements
*   Hopes people had then
*   Problems or failures of that era
*   Feeling, tone
*   Type of leadership most valued then

2. Table groups can then be asked to decide which three items were the most positive and negative influences on the success of the company or institution.

3. The table groups then report to the larger group, and these reports are consolidated on flip charts.

Before going on to the second phase of the Historical Review, the meeting's facilitator can choose an optional enhancement to the Decade Call Out activity. Having fostered a sense of historical movement, it may be helpful to explore our beliefs about the future; what are our biases and what themes do we see emerging in the near future? *These are what we think will happen in the future, not what we want to happen— not our Preferred Future.*

Table groups can spend five to ten minutes describing what they think the world will be like in five years. Each group reports one idea off its list that members think most likely to happen. If time permits, you can go around again. These ideas are listed on flip charts for the entire group to see.

Next, with this picture of the future in front of them, everyone is asked to take ten minutes to contemplate what the total group has said.

People are then asked to shout out words or phrases that help identify themes or trends from the material in front of them. Write these, also, on a chart or overhead. After this, groups would go directly to the scanning activities.

Historical Interview

As shown in the example of the oil company earlier in the chapter, it is often appropriate to identify some of the informal historians who remember how things were. They can be publicly interviewed one by one or in a panel. They can be asked about their memory of significant events, stories, myths, and anecdotes from the past that capture the essence of the organization in the past.

The purpose of the Historical Interview is basically the same as that in the Decade Call Out, but as an additional benefit, it recognizes old-time employees and takes advantage of their special resources— old-timers are helped to shine and be credited and valued for their contributions and knowledge. As a result, everyone develops a sense of the organization's roots.

The Historical Interview involves four steps.

1. The most senior (tenured) member or members can be interviewed, using the same prompting as in Step 1 in the Decade Call Out procedure. This can be done prior to the Preferred Futuring meeting, or preferably during the meeting; if done during the meeting, some rehearsal beforehand is suggested. Also, if there are a sufficient number of old-timers, they can be grouped by the decade in which they joined the organization and interviewed sequentially.

2. As the interview comes to more current decades, others in the meeting (non-old-timers) can be asked to add to or expand on the interviewee's responses.

3. Then small groups can decide on key words or dominant themes of each decade.

4. As in the Decade Call Out activity, these key words or themes are reported out by the table groups to the larger group and documented on flip charts, thus giving the group a historical perspective as it moves forward.

As in the Decade Call Out activity, participants can then go to the second phase of the Historical Review, or they have the option of first working on emergent themes in the same way as described in the Decade Call Out activity.

Time Line Start-Up

The Time Line Start-Up activity is somewhat more interactive and immediate than the prior activities. As illustrated in one of the earlier examples, it begins when the first persons arrive. It sets a tone of participation, creating a personalized picture of the organization's or group's past to determine the themes that characterize its growth and development.

The procedure for this activity is as follows:

1. Before the meeting, a ten- to twenty-foot scroll is placed along a wall of the meeting room. It has the date at which the organization began and is divided up by decades, up to the present.

2. When people arrive they are given Post-it notes and are asked to place their name on the time line at the point they joined the organization. They are also asked to identify significant events in the life of the organization with regard to its growth and development or evolution. These are to be written on Post-it notes and placed on the time line at the appropriate spot. (I worked with one organization that prepared a display of historical pictures and artifacts. This created a lot of interest and reminiscing and helped people think of things to place on the time line.)

3. After the entire group is seated and as it reviews the organization's history, participants can look at this graphic, comment upon it, and suggest themes or patterns in the organization's history. The group then goes to the next phase, the scanning activity.

Review of Past Documentation

If the organization has artifacts and documents that are poignant and relevant to its history, these can be a source of historical data (in the same way as the interviews of old-timers).

This activity has the following procedure:

1. A team is designated that will scan annual reports for the past five or ten years for major historical trends and year-end budget reports for planned versus actual figures. The group will also look at performance data, staffing patterns or levels, brochures, sales materials, major conference agendas, products, and so on.

2. The team looks for and analyzes the themes they see, and reports to the Preferred Futuring meeting on the perspectives that emerge from this theme analysis. Table groups then discuss the material, list the themes they perceive, and call these out to the larger group.

The larger group then goes to the next phase, the scanning activity.

Tools for Scanning History
for Lessons and Consequences

Each of the tools for gathering historical data discussed in the previous sections will help us understand our roots and give a perspective with which to view the present situation of our organization. But we must go further. We must scan the data and explore what we have learned. The past thus provides relevant information for future action and increased sensitivity to the consequences of how past actions guide our future actions.

This scanning phase provides a segue into the next step in the Preferred Futuring model: Identifying Prouds and Sorries. And the results from this scanning process are also used later.

Either of two scanning tools can be chosen, and both are done in table groups:

- Scanning for Relevant Lessons
- Scanning for Consequences

Scanning for Relevant Lessons
To scan the past for relevant lessons involves the following procedure:

1. After the historical data have been gathered and discussed, the entire group is asked to explore their past via call outs of "what we've learned from the past." Some typical lessons:

"In the past we've successfully coped with change and setbacks."
"The organization has been inventive when faced with survival
    issues."
"If we'd taken a longer view, many of our difficulties would have
    been prevented."
"New leadership emerges when needed."
"We have a lot to be proud of."
"It's important to keep an open mind to new markets, techniques,
    and models."

"A lot of what we need to know has already been discovered; if we take the initiative to look for it we can find it."

"It's important to experiment with improvements and change rather than depending on and repeating what has worked before."

"Our past experiences have given us various biases toward future planning. We need to be aware of these and support each other in correcting them."

These lessons can be put on flip charts.

2. Then the group is asked, "What do you want to do with this important knowledge?" This is noted and used later for future planning purposes.

Scanning for Consequences

Scanning the past for consequences is somewhat more personal than scanning for lessons, in that we acknowledge that our actions have led to our current situation, and we state how we would now do things differently.

This activity has the following procedure:

1. Review the data from the historical review.

2. Then ask, "What have we learned from our past?" List the points the group comes up with.

3. Having identified these consequences of our past efforts, participants are asked, "As we think about the future, what are the implications as we plan future actions? And what are the consequences for future actions?" Table groups can brainstorm and discuss ideas under two headings:

• Implications from Past Learnings
• Consequence Sensitivity to Guide Future Actions

These implications and consequences are used later in the futuring process.

The Rules for Brainstorming

Most of you may already know the rules for brainstorming, but because brainstorming will be used so often in the Preferred Futuring process, I am including them for anyone who may not remember them well enough to lead others in brainstorming.

Brainstorming is a method for stimulating creativity and gathering many ideas in a short time. This happens best in an atmosphere where everyone feels free to offer ideas spontaneously, off the top of the head. These rules support that kind of atmosphere:

1. List any idea on the flip chart; repeats are okay.
2. Say everything that comes to mind; no censoring.
3. Permit no discussion; that kills the creative flow.
4. Encourage people to piggyback on other's ideas.
5. Accept and enjoy any moments of silence; often a new and even more creative burst follows.

That's really all there is to it.

Conclusion

Within a Preferred Futuring session, the Historical Review needs to be kept quick and focused. We are quickly touching base with our past to gather relevant perspectives and learnings that will help us determine the future we want. It is a warm-up to exploring the truth about our current situation in greater depth. The results from the Historical Review, posted on the wall or on flip charts, give participants a perspective and a source of data that can be referred to as they go through the rest of the Preferred Futuring process.

4

STEP 2: Identify What's Working and What's Not

Accepting the current situation as it is does not mean we must abandon all hope of improvement and positive change in the future. But it does mean being honest with ourselves and truthful with each other.

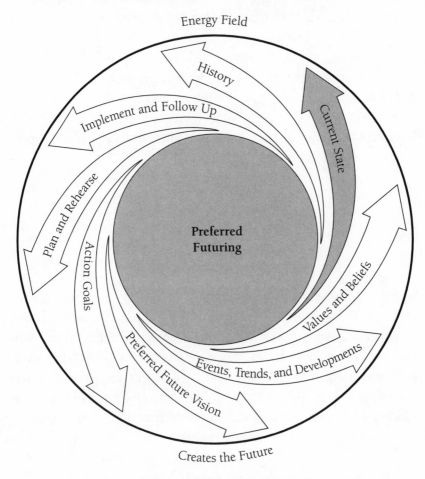

Steps to generate the energy field that manifests the future you want

Figure 4.1   Current State

Assessing Our Current State

Reviewing history, the first step in our path to a Preferred Future, sensitizes us and readies us for exploring how we see what is happening now. And we must assess our present situation before we can explore our preferences for the future. This can be thought of as a scan of current conditions, culture, and structures. It needs to represent a pragmatic view of information useful to the task we want to achieve or the context of the work focus.

Step Two in Preferred Futuring helps build a common database about what we are currently seeing, thinking, and feeling about what is going on in our company, group, or community. This act of data gathering in the context of Preferred Futuring is the task of everyone, not only the so-called experts or the planning group. Thus it is key that all stakeholder perspectives should be seen as relevant. The objective: to create a broad, current, and common perspective.

It is here that Preferred Futuring differs significantly from many problem-solving approaches. When using these other approaches to do an analysis of the current state, it is tempting to list all the problems or things we wish were different—the things we are sorry or mad about. They are after all what's most on our mind. But it is equally important to balance this with what we are proud of or glad about and have been doing right. Our Prouds show competence and strength to build upon, and this balanced approach reduces the tendency to blame and also reduces the negative motivational impact of looking only at problems and focusing only on negative aspects of our situation. (My colleague Kathie Dannemiller sometimes likes to use "glads," "sads," and "mads" instead of Prouds and Sorries as part of her large-scale events. Sometimes this can add more passion and juice to the results, but I think it skews the data in a negative direction.)

Identifying Prouds and Sorries is an extremely powerful part of the Preferred Futuring process for another reason. Many times when people do this step, the information that gets put on the table in the spirit of honest assessment has never been mentioned or discussed except in private—behind closed doors or at the coffee station. Often there is a real sense of catharsis and relief at finally getting it out. At times it can seem like a lot of negative energy, but this in fact releases a lot of positive energy that had been used to keep negative thoughts and feelings submerged or hidden.

 TIP #2: Get widespread involvement in honestly assessing the present and maintain a balanced view of what *is* working as well as what is not working.

Examples of Identifying Prouds and Sorries

The first example below shows how Prouds and Sorries are identified, and the second shows the flexibility of the Preferred Futuring process—how stakeholders can be integrated into the process.

Phew, Not as Bad as We Thought

Three hundred senior to midlevel leaders and managers are seated at tables of eight, with each table representing a microcosm of the organization—a maximum mixture of disciplines and levels represented at the event. Their purpose: redefine the company's core business, its mission, its strategies, and develop a plan for carrying these out.

Using suggested categories like "how have we been meeting our customer needs" and "how have we been working together," the participants at each table are asked to call out what they are proud about and what they are sorry about in the current organizational situation. At first the groups are a little slow in starting, but within ten minutes the fervor and energy around each table is very high. Things only muttered at the coffee machine or after hours are being shared openly across organizational boundaries in a constructive and structured way.

Table leaders and designated recorders capture these Prouds and Sorries on flip charts in brainstorming fashion. Next each table is asked to discuss the list for about thirty minutes and agree on the top three items in each list, the sorriest Sorries and the proudest Prouds. Then tables report out their top items, which are recorded centrally. This creates a lot of face-to-face exchange of views in a smaller and safer table setting, and it also establishes a common database across the whole meeting—and the whole organization.

During this step, lots of tough information comes out about dissatisfaction with leadership, other departments, and work processes and about the lack of common standards across the whole system. But there is a sense of relief that the situation isn't as bad as was feared. There is also a sense that "we are doing some things right."

Involving Stakeholders

An engineering organization is holding a two-day strategic alignment off-site with the top third of its organization. It is break time, just after Prouds and Sorries have been established. Representatives of customer organizations, who had not been in the prior session, are being briefed on what had happened during the last part of the meeting. They also receive a final briefing about their role: as a panel, when the session is reconvened, they will be asked to present their lists of Glads and Sads (the customer's equivalent to the Prouds and Sorries mentioned earlier) with regard to this organization's performance.

This panel discussion goes as planned, and afterward the table groups review what they think they heard and what questions need to be asked for deeper understanding.

The customers later comment that they really feel listened to. Most of them volunteer to be available for further discussions as needed.

The meeting allows the organization's staff, working without customers (stakeholders), to identify Prouds and Sorries. It then also allows customers to be fully involved, with their input integrated into the final information.

Tools for Identifying Prouds and Sorries

There is one basic tool used for identifying Prouds and Sorries, but several additional tools can enhance this step.

How to Identify Prouds and Sorries

Remember, the purpose here is to identify what's working and what's not. Identifying Prouds and Sorries involves the following procedure.

1. Participants are sitting in table groups, with each table group being a microcosm of the organization to the maximum degree possible given attendance at the event.

2. They are briefed on the importance of honesty and speaking their truth.

3. Each table group has a designated recorder and a flip chart.

4. The instructions to the groups are: "Knowing what you know about this organization [community, or whatever name is appropriate] with regard to [put in the specific focus of the meeting, such as quality of work life, customer satisfaction, work processes, and so on], what are you most proud of and what are you sorriest about. List these on your flip charts."

5. When the groups are done, they go back and clarify the items and identify the three proudest Prouds and sorriest Sorries at each table.

6. Tables are then polled for their priority items and a total system perspective is created.

Like the results from the Historical Review, the results of the Prouds and Sorries exercise are put on flip chart pages and taped to the wall, or typed up and distributed by a designated documenter and logistics team; in this way the results become part of the group's database as it moves forward in the Preferred Futuring model.

Alternative Instructions

In Steps 4 and 5 in the basic procedure, an alternative set of instructions can be given to participants at each table. "Pretend you are in a helicopter, or on a flying carpet, looking down—this week—on your organization [community, whatever]. Call out your concrete observations of what you see or hear going on that makes you proud and pleased or sorry and displeased. Record the result of this brainstorming session on your flip chart at each table, splitting the sheet between these two categories." Then identify the three proudest Prouds and sorriest Sorries.

After this (and if you have the time), you can get a deeper understanding of Step Two in the Preferred Futuring process and how it is linked to Step One by starting a discussion based on the following questions:

- Is there a relationship between these Prouds and Sorries of the present and the evaluations of history that we made earlier?
- Are there some implications that seem to emerge from these priority Sorries?
- Have we ever really celebrated our priority Prouds?

If Steps 4 and 5 in the procedure use these alternative instructions, Step 6 remains the same: the results from each table are consolidated into a report for the overall group.

An Optional Warm-Up Exercise
Prior to going through the procedure to identify Prouds and Sorries, it may be helpful to go through a warm-up exercise that increases the group's sensitivity to the characteristics of the organization or system and its world. This may also help people to label their perceptions about the system and legitimize and share feelings.

This activity has the following procedure:

1. People from the entire organization or system are sitting in table groups.

2. Each participant has a checklist containing adjectives and phrases that might describe their observations and feeling about the organization (or community or some other system). A checklist might look like this:

Observations About the Organization	*Feelings About the Organization*
Organized	Loyal
Authoritarian	Discouraged
Disorganized	Alienated
Democratic	Resistant
Important	Noninfluential
Laissez-faire	Exploited
Innovative	Proud
Productive	Ashamed
Inflexible	
Competitive	
Obsolete	
Collaborative	

3. Participants take an observer posture (from outside the organization) and circle the words that best state their observations and feelings, or those of others, about the organization. They are urged to write in any additional observations and feelings that seem relevant.

4. Table groups then review the words that they identified most frequently, and put a (+) or a (−) next to those observations and feelings deemed as positive or negative.

5. Table groups then write a descriptive sentence about the organization for each of the most frequently mentioned words.

6. This information is then shared across the whole group for discussion and agreement.

This activity can put participants in the right mood to identify Prouds and Sorries. And the checklist may give participants ideas about Prouds and Sorries.

Involving Customers and Other Stakeholders in This Process

Preferred Futuring offers flexibility not only as to whether customers and other stakeholders participate in identifying Prouds and Sorries, but offers two common ways in which they can participate.

The first way was shown in the example of the engineering organization earlier in this chapter, and involves the following procedure:

1. Invited representatives of major customer or stakeholder groups are oriented to their role prior to the Preferred Futuring event and told how their participation will fit into the larger context.

2. At the event they can be seated as a panel and interviewed about Glads and Sads from their point of view.

3. Then they can be asked to comment on needs they anticipate having in the future and what this implies for their future relationship with this organization.

4. There can be a question-and-answer session in a large gathering, or relevant subgroups of the organization can question stakeholders in detail in simultaneous break-out sessions.

Second, customers or other stakeholders can be invited to participate in the Prouds and Sorries session at tables alongside members of the host organization. This often feels more risky on the part of the host organization. The risk (and benefit) is that it may take everyone to a new level of openness and build trust.

After either type of stakeholder involvement, their input is integrated into the common database.

Conclusion

After Prouds and Sorries have been identified, I have noticed that the feeling in the room or the system is not the same as before this step. I have never tested the hypothesis, but I believe that if the process were to stop here, there would be markedly noticeable differences in the system just because Prouds and Sorries had been honestly shared; the creation of this common database is that powerful. Identifying Prouds and Sorries and Reviewing History provide a solid base and develop a shared spirit that permeates the rest of the Preferred Futuring process.

5

STEP 3: Identify Values and Beliefs

This is critical: we have to decide what kind of future we prefer. This gets us down to the tough questions about what we value and what we really want. . . . We have to know what our intentions are. Many of us have never been taught to think this way.

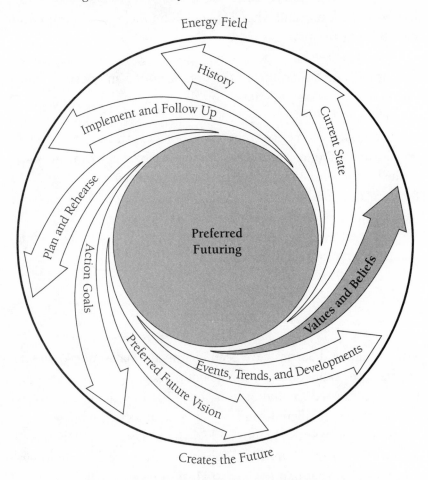

Energy Field

History

Implement and Follow Up

Current State

Plan and Rehearse

Action Goals

Preferred
Futuring

Values and Beliefs

Preferred Future Vision

Events, Trends, and Developments

Creates the Future

Steps to generate the energy field that manifests the future you want

Figure 5.1 Values and Beliefs

How Values and Beliefs Can Determine Our Reality

In junior high school I once wrote an essay titled "Values: The Rudder of Life," for which I got a high mark. I still think the metaphor is a good one. Further experience, since then, has convinced me that our values and beliefs directly affect what we do create for ourselves. For example, if I believe I don't deserve something, I probably won't create it in my life. I believe the same is true on a collective basis in all human systems—organizational or community, nationwide or worldwide.

Therefore, to create even greater and more wonderful realities in our future, it is very important to assess our beliefs and values and be willing to scrutinize and modify them if need be. Certainly we have values about change as good or bad, or good for others and bad for us, and so on. We have values about people as most important or profit as most important. We have values or beliefs about the efficacy or destructiveness of authoritarian (top-down) versus democratic (participative, team-based) organizational structures, leadership processes, and organizational culture.

In 1970 at the National Organization Development Conference, I remember that a hot topic was whether to consult or not to consult with organizations that built bombs that burned women and children or otherwise supported the worldwide, war-based economic structure. Some people said that it was wrong to help these organizations. Others said that it was important to work within these organizations to help them realistically assess what they were doing. What I remember is that it was the open dialogue that really mattered. It allowed us all to explore and clarify our own values and beliefs, to influence and be influenced.

In the early 1970s there was an explosion of interest in values clarification, with workshops and books about activities to do in the community, the classroom, and the boardroom. Louis Raths and then Sid Simon (University of Massachusetts) pioneered this area; many of the models and activities can be found in books by these two men and many others.[1] I see the interest in values coming around again. In the last two or three years, increased attention is being paid to such things as values-based management and values-based missions with guiding principles.

 TIP #3: Be sure to surface and explore core values and beliefs for deeper meaning, richer understanding, and clearer focus. Don't leave out this step.

The primary objective in identifying values and beliefs is to understand what determined past patterns, achievements, or mistakes (the Historical Review and Prouds and Sorries). It is also important to surface and explore underlying values and beliefs that will determine how we approach the future together, and clarify values or attitudes about holding on to or letting go of the past. Skipping this step will deprive the organization of the chance to review and connect with its guiding principles and articulate them in relation to the mission. Alignment at the level of values and beliefs is very helpful as an organization moves toward the future. And yet this step has too often been forgotten by those rushing to get to the vision (as if it was only a product), or left out due to executive pressure to reduce the time that the whole Preferred Futuring process takes.

Example of Determining Values and Beliefs

The director of a large Midwestern state department of transportation wants to change the leadership style and culture of his department. But he sees his leadership team as entrenched in traditional management beliefs and attitudes. He thinks a futuring event will help his team identify core values regarding leadership currently in use in a context of the organization's needs as it moves into the future. Discussing this topic and openly sharing ideas about it have been avoided up to now.

At the futuring event, the group is deeply engrossed in sharing what new type of leadership their organization needs. They are following rules of dialogue that allow a free flow of personal beliefs and opinions with no judgment, and there is no context of having to make a decision. One facilitator periodically helps them keep to the rules. The other one is writing madly on a flip chart pad that is faced away from the leadership team. The energy in their voices increases and the comments become more deeply meaningful and thoughtful.

After a period of fifty to sixty minutes the facilitators call a halt. After a break, the facilitators report back the key points, values, beliefs, and principles that were mentioned in the discussion. Several flip chart pages are covered. The leadership team sits in stunned silence. Then participants make comments about the profound ideas on the charts, the depth and openness of the discussion, and how rewarding it was to spend time together talking in this way.

This material provided core elements for the new role of manager in this organization. The leadership team handed off a clear set of general guidelines to a team that was a microcosm of the organization, and this team created the "101 ways" to fulfill the new role of manager in this organization, a role that included being a developer and supporter of people, culture, organization, and productivity—values identified in the meeting.

This definition of leadership based on future-oriented core values became the basis of a future vision for leadership throughout the department, which all section leaders, managers, and supervisors agreed to align with. The system became structurally changed when these principles and specific behavioral descriptions became the criteria for yearly performance reviews and for interviewing prospective employees. The culture and leadership style did shift.

Tools for Determining Core Values and Beliefs

Either of two tools can be used to identify Core Values and Beliefs:

- Value Forming, Sharing, and Clarifying
- Scanning for Core Values

Value Forming, Sharing, and Clarifying

Value Forming, Sharing, and Clarifying uses the following procedure:

1. Each participant takes five 3″ × 5″ cards.

2. Participants are asked to write on each card a belief or value that guides their decision making and behavior. For example, if participants are teachers or trainers, they would list beliefs that guide behavior toward students or trainees.

3. Then participants look over their own cards and decide which belief is the most *important* one for them, that is, the one they'd be least willing to give up. These cards are to be marked with an "I" for important.

4. They then mark with a "V" the belief they find themselves violating most frequently, that is, the one they have the most trouble living up to.

5. Then people form trios, put all of their cards side by side, read one another's cards, and:

- Identify similarities and differences.
- Probe each other on reasons for differences that interest them.
- Explore in some detail the reasons for and difficulties with violating the "V" values.

6. Then each person considers whether to include or emphasize in their top values any of the values identified by other people.

7. Participants then report their most interesting learnings and discoveries to the total group.

8. After these values and beliefs are shared, the group determines the major themes and things learned—the values we want to hold on to as we move into the future.

Scanning for Core Values

As an alternative to the Value Forming, Sharing, and Clarifying activity, you can Scan for Core Values, using the following procedure:

1. Participants in table groups are given a set of categories that organize their memories about the organization's history. These categories typically involve economic or financial data, leadership information, key decisions or policies, milestones, accomplishments, and so on.

2. The participants are then asked to check with each other on which categories are the most significant and why. This will get at underlying beliefs and values.

3. They are asked a final question: "What are the core values and beliefs that we want to take into the future?"

4. Table groups report their results to the group, and common core values are identified.

Optional Tools for Identifying Values and Beliefs

In addition to the tools for identifying core values, there are two optional tools that can enhance this process:

- Scanning for Values and Beliefs Basic to Future Thinking
- Scanning for a Static or Dynamic Value System

Scanning for Values and Beliefs Basic to Future Thinking

After identifying core values, it may become clear that the organization is having difficulty in letting go of cherished ideas that might block creation of a transformative Preferred Future image. In this case you can develop criteria with which to evaluate these values and practices and better decide which to keep.

Using the data from the Historical Review and Prouds and Sorries activities, this optional activity has the following steps:

1. Table groups clarify the criteria each member was using to define a Proud or a Sorry. This way of treating Prouds and Sorries allows values criteria to emerge.

2. From these criteria, the table groups can discuss the values underlying these criteria, as well as use the criteria to ratify the core values previously identified.

3. Then these values are reported out to the general meeting for discussion.

4. Finally, the overall group agrees on a set of guiding values and beliefs.

Scanning for a Static or Dynamic Value System

As an optional warm-up activity, before using either of the tools for identifying core values, it may be helpful to see whether your organization has a static or dynamic value system—a difference that will influence its attitude as it goes through this step in the Preferred Futuring process.

This activity is done at the Preferred Futuring event and has the following procedure:

1. Each table group brainstorms examples of programs, events, policies, or media coverage that have occurred in the past year, looking for examples that fall into any of the following categories:

- Risk taking
- Initiating
- Adapting
- Adjusting
- Maintaining

2. Table groups are then asked, "What values have been expressed in those events?" This gives a quick picture from which basic value postures can be identified. These values are also recorded on a flip chart for review. They form the starting point for identifying core values and beliefs using the tools discussed earlier.

Conclusion

Our beliefs determine our initiatives to create a future. What we assume that future will be like influences our expectations of the consequences and the risks we take. So it is very important for us to explore our assumptions and clarify the values that underlie these assumptions.

To get ready to make informed collective decisions about our preferred future, it is first necessary to explore what we believe about ourselves and our organization or community. This step gives us a common awareness, a common values base with which to go forward.

6

STEP 4: Identify Relevant Events, Developments, and Trends

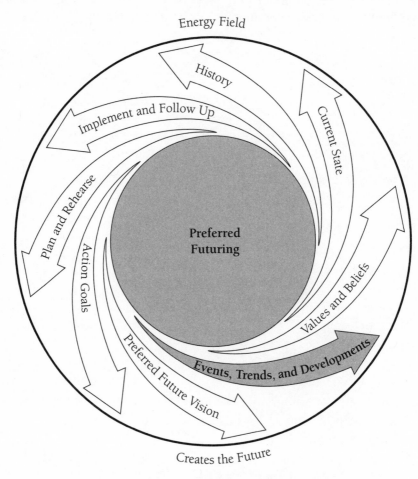

Steps to generate the energy field that manifests the future you want

Figure 6.1 Events, Trends, and Developments

White horse clip-clopping
Over the moonlit field
Oh
I'm part of the picture
—HAIKU BY BASHO

Scanning the Horizon

It is a very basic shift in orientation to move from being an observer or analyst—someone who reflects about what is going on in the world of our organization or community—to becoming an actor, goal setter, and doer—part of the picture. To be in the posture of an intelligent doer regarding our future, we must discover an important source of information: awareness of the current events out there in the world, the trends that are taking shape and the developments that may affect us on our way to the future. As we formulate our Preferred Future vision and our action plans to achieve that vision, these events, trends, and developments must be taken into account.

 TIP #4: Scanning the horizon for events, developments, and trends should involve everyone.

Scanning is a different activity from typical data gathering. It involves a survey of personal, subjective experiences as well as expert, objective data. It includes getting small, focused, easily digestible bits of information representing events, trends, or developments—things that are just coming over the horizon, such as developments in technology, marketplace changes, legislation or regulation changes, recent company policy decisions, societal or global trends. We must consider these so they don't blindside us on our way to the future.

Examples of Identifying
Events, Developments, and Trends

The examples in this section illustrate how a group's familiarity with the subject will determine the types of information it accesses, and how important it is to get a broad range of information representing different perspectives and different people.

Instilling a Sense of Urgency

Five hundred leaders and managers who represent the whole top of a large health care organization are seated in a ballroom at tables of twelve. Each table includes people of different ranks and from different parts of the total organization. They are here to plan a rapid and deep realignment of their whole organization, a realignment needed to stay competitive even though there is no shared sense of urgency about it in the organization.

It is the first day of a three-day futuring event, and the ballroom is abuzz with the results of the Prouds and Sorries and Values exploration activities. The mood in the room has shifted because for the first time a common database has been created about how people honestly view the situation. There is an air of higher energy and animated conversations. Now each table group brainstorms on all the events, developments, and trends shaping or soon to shape the organization's actions. They consider new or pending federal legislation, new technology or practices in the field, public attitudes and needs as well as events, developments, and trends (ED&Ts) within their organization such as pending policies, program changes, and so forth.

Then each table discusses the lists and decides on the three ED&Ts that will have the most positive or negative impact on the organization. These data are summarized, and top leadership then adds its views corroborating or adding to the ED&Ts identified.

It is obvious that a new and growing sense of urgency has been established in the room. The leadership team is so excited that it's difficult to keep them focused on the next steps in the process—attaching this new sense of urgency to strategic goals and objectives that will be supported by all five hundred leaders and managers.

Scanning the Horizon

When one hospital began examining ED&Ts as part of the Preferred Futuring process, it discovered that its staff was not knowledgeable enough on the ED&Ts affecting them. So, for one month all the employees became ED&T scanners. Everyone in the organization was asked to scan newspapers, comic strips, news weeklies or monthlies, trade journals, strategic planning documents, future trend books and articles, electronic bulletin boards, and the customers with whom they came in contact or other key informants.

They pooled the data with an ED&T coordinating group. This group presented the ED&T data at the next futuring event. The report stimulated widespread involvement in and attention to the strategic visioning and action planning process. The group could then move on in the Preferred Futuring process.

So successful was this way of gathering and disseminating data about ED&Ts that it was adopted as part of the hospital's regular planning process.

Tools for Examining
Events, Developments, and Trends

There is one basic tool for examining ED&Ts, but as will be shown, there are various ways for assembling the information about the ED&Ts.

Identifying ED&Ts involves the following procedure.

1. Designate a flip chart recorder for each table.

2. Introduce an example of an ED&T, and explain the task and why ED&Ts are important. Then set the table groups to work on Steps 3 through 5 of this procedure for twenty to thirty minutes.

3. Table groups brainstorm and record all ED&Ts, including stakeholders and governmental, political, economic, technological, social, and environmental issues both internal and external to the organization, that may have an impact on it in the future. These are captured on the flip chart.

4. Table groups review these ED&Ts and identify the three that may have the most positive impact and the top three that may have the most negative impact as the organization moves into the future. The groups use a (+) or (−) to indicate anticipated positive or negative impact.

5. Give table groups a five-minute warning, then call the whole group to order. Ask for reports on key ED&Ts from each table. A good process is to call for one (+) and (−) ED&T from each table so the first table report does not steal the thunder of other tables. Record the reported items on a master flip chart.

6. End with a review of the key trends reported and a summary of the implications for future actions.

The end result: The ED&Ts and their positive and negative implications are recorded on flip charts or on the wall. Like the Historical Review, Prouds and Sorries, and Values and Beliefs, they become part of the group's solid foundation as it goes forward in the Preferred Futuring process.

Assembling Information About ED&Ts

In the procedure just discussed, ED&Ts are derived from brainstorming. In the hospital example earlier in the chapter, participants prepared for this step by scanning various sources of data. There are other ways to prime the pump and prepare participants for examining ED&Ts.

First, give specific guidelines and instructions. Before the meeting, participants can be assigned the task of preparing a small brief containing their major ED&Ts inside and outside the organization, ED&Ts that are affecting it now and will continue to do so in the future. Participants also identify the implications of these ED&Ts for the organization.

Second, a planning or leadership team can collect a variety of short statements about future trends by expert futurists or from other sources. The team can distribute these one- or two-page articles or simple tables and graphs to table groups at the futuring event. This material is read, and then people discuss it and the implications for the future of their department, organization, or community.

Both these preparatory activities allow people to participate more fully and intelligently during this step in the process.

Conclusion

This step does not have to take very long, but it is important because it helps prepare each person in the whole organization to be a strategic thinking planner and implementer. It prepares us to take our journey into the future and create our Preferred Future—and do this more wisely.

7

STEP 5: Create a Preferred Future Vision

You see things and say why, but I dream of things and say why not.
—GEORGE BERNARD SHAW

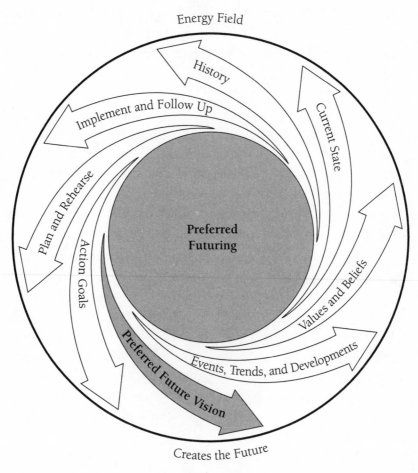

Energy Field

History

Implement and Follow Up

Current State

Plan and Rehearse

Action Goals

Preferred Futuring

Values and Beliefs

Preferred Future Vision

Events, Trends, and Developments

Creates the Future

Steps to generate the energy field that manifests the future you want

Figure 7.1 Preferred Future Vision

My interest in the future is because I'm going to spend the rest of my life there.

—Charles F. Kettering

What Future Do I Prefer?

Based on the steps in Chapters Three through Six, we have now answered the questions, What has led us to be where we are now? What is going on now in our world? and What might happen in our world? In Step Five we now ask people to move into an action posture and ask, What do I or we feel passionately enough about to make happen? or What future would we prefer? This requires discipline, commitment, and a sense of adventure.

As I have already pointed out, Preferred Futuring initiates a large paradigm shift, taking us from being powerless victims to being empowered and connected to our deep passions and motivated to work together to create the future we want. It means we are responsible and can't blame others. But there is a tendency to resist this reality. For many of us, feeling helpless or victimized has been a way of coping with our sense of powerlessness. By staying vague and uncommitted, we avoid the risk of being disappointed if things don't work out the way we want. In fact we may believe that it is best to let things happen, and feel freer and more able to be spontaneous about whatever comes up. Letting go of these old notions is part of creating the future.

Asking the question, What future do I prefer? shifts the window that we look through. I got a call from a colleague who is an internal consultant in a major software company, known to us all. She was working with product work teams in a very rapid and intense environment. When a version of software was issued, teams would be mobilized to learn from customer feedback and update the product with customer-driven improvements. She found teams that were demoralized by all the negative feedback. She asked teams to envision the next generation of product, operating just the way they think it should. This invariably shifted each team into high energy and creative, out-of-the-box thinking that resulted in quicker cycle time and greater increments of product improvement. She was so excited about the results, she had to call me right away!

If we develop a preferred future before we plan, there is a greater chance of getting the future we want and of operating as a whole system. There is a greater chance of avoiding fragmentation, suboptimization, drifting, and loss of energy. In fact we are freer when we plan proactively than when we just react. Through the Preferred Futuring process, people learn to believe in their hearts and souls that all of us benefit by projecting and assessing the future we collectively want, and by working together to create it.

This step for creating the Preferred Future vision typically yields up a profound document of six to twelve strategic priorities, with specific descriptions of what each of these future conditions looks like. Think of these strategic priorities as components of the vision. Put another way, a preferred vision consists of several images.

This document may be six to thirty-six pages long. It becomes the guiding vision and the source of criteria for success, so progress can be measured. And it contains the passion, dreams, and heart of the organization or community as a whole system.

 TIP #5: The image of a Preferred Future must be specific and detailed.

I recently worked with a small but key unit of a large worldwide energy company. They wanted to build a new team with their new manager, and align around an agreed-upon mission, vision, and guiding principles and goals. What they called their vision was a one-liner. It could have been another version of the mission. It was not a detailed description of where they were going. They lacked a well-articulated Preferred Future statement. They had a hard time seeing that they needed to go beyond their one-line vision and articulate a full Preferred Future image. We need to be clear what we mean by our vision of the future; to me, *vision* means a Preferred Future vision, as the next example illustrates.

Example of Creating a Preferred Future Vision

To become more cost-effective and responsive to customers, a state department of transportation had adopted quality as its strategy. Its mission was to "provide the highest quality transportation services to support economic growth and increased quality of life" in the state.

In a Preferred Futuring event, leaders, managers, and supervisors were seated at tables to develop their Preferred Future vision of an excellent transportation department. Each person had written down answers to the following questions: What does the future look like three years from now? How are you working in cross-functional teams to meet internal and external customer demands? What are your customers saying? What are legislators saying? What is the state of the statewide transportation infrastructure that really pleases you and tells you that we have truly become a high-quality organization and are successfully implementing our mission?

The answers to these questions were images of the individual's Preferred Future vision of quality transportation service. Here is a sample of the images from one table, images that were listed on the table's flip chart:

- Customer data is being collected, collated, analyzed, and interpreted into accurate and measurable information, which is available to all via our strategic data system.
- Customers are served using a known process, which is adhered to and accepted, and teams maintain and control their own processes.
- A manager is heard asking a team "how can I help you?" rather than "how soon can you do it?"
- The leadership team is lending strong support by collaborating directly with teams and committees, and they provide coaching and advice, but leave "the doing" to us.
- Traffic fatalities are 50 percent lower than in 1993, according to a published newspaper article.
- There is a plan, based on employee input that has intermediate (two- and five-year) plans and short-term goals.

Each table's images were posted onto a master list, and the entire group voted, selecting nine priority image statements, some of which were:

- Placing concern for all customers first, last, and always.
- Ensuring that people are regarded as our most important asset.
- Having made quality the strategy to improve service, quality continues to be the solution to our problems.
- Eliminating fear in the workplace.
- Emphasizing teamwork and knowledge sharing in everything we do.

Each of these priority image statements had a collection of other specific images listed under it defining what it meant. For the first statement, "Placing concern for all customers first, last, and always," some of the specific images were:

Customer data is being collected, collated, analyzed, and interpreted into accurate and measurable information and is available to all via our strategic data systems.

Customer data is being used in meetings throughout our department for quality improvement.

The customer database indicates that overall complaints are down by 90 percent.

- Complaints from partners such as road builders are approaching zero.
- We conduct public relations activities including tours of department facilities.

For the fourth statement, "Eliminating fear in the workplace," some of the specific images were:

All leaders and managers are focusing on coaching and removing blocks.

People are not blamed, they are separated from the problem.

Candid discussions are encouraged and are taking place, discussions that identify obstacles and create solutions for reducing inefficiency.

Mutual trust and respect is evident as people across disciplines and ranks really listen to each other.

All leaders and managers share basic beliefs that:

- People want to do a quality job.
- People have many good ideas that can benefit the department.
- People want to be contributing members of a winning team.
- People want to give trust and commitment, but these can only be earned.
- People prefer to cooperate and support each other's successes, rather than compete and block success.

As you can see, the priority vision statement, when typed, is not a one-line or even one-paragraph statement, but will take up several pages. It includes success criteria and other material for use in the remainder of the Preferred Futuring process: formulating action goals, interim goals (if necessary), and action steps that include specific first steps. As each team works on one of these priority vision statements, all the underlying images provide specific direction for implementation and evaluation.

Tools for Developing a Preferred Future Vision

Creating a Preferred Future Vision is a three-phase process:

- *Phase 1:* Warm-Up Exercise
- *Phase 2:* Taking the Trip
- *Phase 3:* Voting on Preferred Visions

Phase 1: Warm-Up Exercise

This activity helps people think in the future tense and create a specific Preferred Future image, because sometimes people need to get the feel of it first. But this phase can be optional if the Preferred Futuring facilitator believes people are ready for the real thing.

This activity has the following procedure:

1. From Steps One through Four in the Preferred Futuring process, a small group develops several kinds of summary data, which might be under headings like:

- What we want to be sure not to repeat
- What we want to let go of
- What we want to be from now on
- How we want to be different in the future from how we have been in the past
- What we want to build on or hold on to as we create our future
- Our proudest Prouds and sorriest Sorries
- The most important ED&Ts we have identified

The intention is to recall all the multifaceted perspectives and ideas, so we can think creatively and comprehensively about the future we want.

2. This summary data is hung on the walls on flip chart sheets or typed and distributed to table groups.

3. The total group is informed that they are a commission in the year 2000 preparing a report to be opened in the year 2500. The sheets on the wall are the chapters of the report. Teams are assigned to write each chapter, consisting of one or two pages and taking about fifteen minutes. They describe how things are in the year 2010, things that are important and noteworthy to share with their descendants in the year 2500.

This is a skill development activity that readies participants to take the trip into Preferred Futuring.

Phase 2: Taking the Trip
Taking the Trip helps people let go, get out of the box, think more globally and from a systems perspective as they create their Preferred

Future. Participants will be stretched to consider their current organization or community situation in a larger global context. The trip will also help them consider how the wider environment may influence them, what impact they want to have on it, and how to become aligned with a set of strategic priorities connected to a wider systems view. Participants are told, "In this project, you have the opportunity to try out the role of the futurist—with an individual futuring project." The procedure is as follows:

The trip must begin with a decision about how far into the future to travel. Participants are then given the following instructions:

1. Take a piece of paper and a pen, relax and be comfortable, and ignore the others around you. This can be done at the table where participants are sitting.

2. In your head, go forward to the future date—you are there, looking down on your situation from a balloon with X-ray vision and enhanced hearing, so you can see and hear everything that is going on.

3. Make descriptive observations in the present tense on your paper of what you see and hear going on in the organization that please you—activities, relationships, policies, communications, decisions, attitudes, and so on. Write down what really pleases you and indicates that the efforts we began today (use the current date) were totally successful in bringing about the changes necessary for complete success. [The instruction above is generic; the specific instruction would be based on the context of the situation—the purpose of the meeting. And instructions can be more structured, with individuals being asked to make their observations under these headings: My World, My Community, My Country, My Organization, Me. This step should take about ten minutes.

Don't prioritize these observations; the purpose of this step is simply to generate ideas—generate images. But describe what you see and hear as specifically and concretely as you can.

4. Present these images to your table group. Consolidate everyone's images on a master list, but don't lose specificity.

5. The lists are posted for the entire group to see. And Phase 3 begins.

Phase 3: Voting on Strategic Priorities

As mentioned earlier in this chapter, a Preferred Vision consists of several preferred images or strategic priorities, each of which are further defined by several specific images. Voting on strategic priorities helps participants quickly determine the collective strategic focus or alignment to which they feel commitment. They are thus in a position to move into action planning and implementation in a direction that excites them. This activity sets strategic priorities that are connected with people's passion and creativity. Anyone with really creative or "out there" thinking has a chance to influence and stretch the entire organization.

After table groups have posted their preferred images, everyone is given five sticky dots and one gold star. The instructions are:

1. Read all the preferred images from all the groups, including your own.

2. Place your five dots on the images you feel most passionate about, those that will make the biggest difference in the right direction.

3. Place your star on the one image you feel so passionate about that "if this one doesn't happen . . . forget the whole thing!"

Then participants take a break while a representative task force of five people compiles the results. These are presented to the entire group for final ratification. The high vote-getters will be the strategic priorities around which you will develop Action Plans.

When you review the results and make your final decision about strategic priorities, if some starred items didn't make the final list, then those who voted with the star get a chance to explain their reasons. This may give some really creative future thinker a chance to influence the rest of the system. When these people are heard, very often their starred item gets subsumed under a designated priority item or a new priority item is established.

Conclusion

The result of this step is a Preferred Future Vision, consisting of several strategic priorities, each of which is defined by detailed images of success.

The total Preferred Futuring process includes steps beyond this one to assure follow-up and successful results—turning the Vision into Goals and creating an Action Plan to achieve those Goals. These further steps also are based on sound change theory, research, and the wisdom of experience. Of course, it is important that general follow-up activities and structure be identified and committed to by leadership before beginning the Preferred Futuring process.

At this moment, a lot of energy for action has been mobilized. Yet this is a vulnerable point in the change process. To be successful, this energy needs to become focused, directed, and supported. The next steps in the Preferred Futuring process provide ways to achieve this.

8

STEP 6: Translate Future Visions into Action Goals

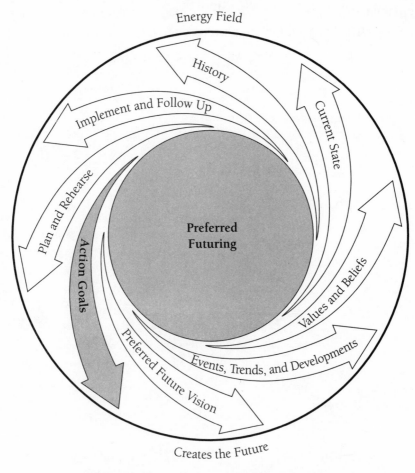

Energy Field

History

Implement and Follow Up

Current State

Plan and Rehearse

Preferred
Futuring

Action Goals

Values and Beliefs

Preferred Future Vision

Events, Trends, and Developments

Creates the Future

Steps to generate the energy field that manifests the future you want

Figure 8.1 Action Goals

Immediately, future hope and expectation begin to change your present. As you contemplate the future, something very magical happens. You are immediately transported back to the present. You are now forced to contemplate the impact of your present actions on that Preferred Future.

Going from Intention to Action

When we translate a Preferred Future vision consisting of several strategic priorities and images into action goals, we are presented with the challenge of a universal question: Should we really put energy and commitment into a desired future? Many of us grew up in educational systems where we were graded for knowing the right answers, not for our motivation or skills to carry them out. In this even more complex world, it has become easy to resist the impulse to action with comments like "It won't be feasible" or "It will cost too much" or "It is too idealistic" or "It is not practical" or "There is not enough support" or "It is too soon" or "It is too risky"—and as we know, the list can go on and on.

We all have stories and experiences of how training or major organization-change programs have led to very little carryover into action or led to unmet business objectives. This is the real challenge: how do we plan and organize to take action—how do we put legs on the vision?

The key to successful implementation is, of course, early involvement of the implementers in the vision and plan. The Preferred Futuring process is a powerful tool for accomplishing this involvement.

 TIP #6: Be sure to pay close attention to and provide quality time for translating the Preferred Future vision into action goals and then action plans.

Example of Translating Future Vision into Action Goals

The setting is a Preferred Futuring town meeting. Over several months, Preferred Future images have been collected from all citizens and this input has been summarized into vision statements, and the highest-priority image statements for the city's Preferred Future vision have been selected. One of these statements calls for a river waterfront that adds beauty and attractiveness to the city. This originated from many Sorry statements about the polluted and trashed-out river area that runs through the town and the wish to turn this into an asset for quality of life and attractiveness for tourism and business. This priority image statement is supported by several action goals, all seen as effective within the next ten years:

The Strategic Priority and Specific Image Statements

The Strategic Priority: Our riverfront is clean, with natural landscaping in many areas, and is an asset to our community, enhancing both quality of life and our economy

Specific Image Statements (to be turned into goals):
- The river is clean enough to swim and fish in.
- The city maintains two riverfront parks that include public facilities and public shelters where many annual public and private events can take place, and all facilities are user-friendly and accessible to the handicapped.
- The riverfront has a privately operated canoe livery.
- A bike and jogging trail flows all along the riverbank, from one end of town to the other, with access to public businesses.
- The riverfront is featured in our chamber of commerce literature.

Thus an image statement now becomes a series of action goal statements, each with specific details explaining what it means. These can later be used to create objectives and criteria for success.

The Tools for Translating Future Vision into Action Goals

Translating Preferred Future visions into action goals is a two-phase process:

- Phase 1. Setting Criteria
- Phase 2. Forming Action Goals

Both phases are done by teams of volunteers that form around a specific preferred image that particularly excites them, and these "Goal Development" teams then operate as planning groups.

Phase 1: Setting Criteria

Sometimes it is difficult to decide which of our preferred images under each strategic priority should become goals for action. The following criteria are often useful in doing this:

- Are there clear priority payoffs to this image?
- Will the image be feasible to attain?
- Is the level of risk in trying to reach the image acceptable?
- Does the image invoke a sense of challenge?
- Will this image be of interest to others, and will they be able to get involved?
- Will the image allow a logical movement toward where we want to go and help achieve the strategic priority?
- Does this image lend itself to pilot possibilities?
- Is this image instrumental to other goals or strategic priorities?

In addition to these criteria, think of some that fit your specific situation. The final list of criteria is used in Phase 2 of this step.

Phase 2: Forming Action Goals

To implement the preferred images identified in Chapter Five, you must develop clear and specific outcomes for each and concrete plans to achieve these outcomes. These outcomes take the form of two or three action statements (goals) that can be used for action planning.

To begin the action planning process, goal development teams are given the following instructions:

1. List all the concrete clues or examples describing what it looks like if the image is achieved, especially what could be measured or

observed by someone—flesh out your preferred image. Create as specific an image as possible.

2. Then convert your image into an action statement with several action goals. To help in this process, consider the criteria that you developed earlier.

3. Then ask another group to consult. Share your overall image and specific examples. The other group's job is to ask questions, probe, clarify, and give additional examples. In return, help them in the same way. This is a critical step. Don't rush through it.

After this step in the Preferred Futuring model, each goal development team has a complete picture of its goal. And the organization has a set of final goals.

Conclusion

This Preferred Futuring step generates lots of motivation, which helps propel the organization into active and unified implementation. The point of translating visions into goals is that the effort starts you down the road to implementation. Ideas must converge to support implementation. Keep the tasks simple and quick. This is not the time for "dotting the I's and crossing the t's."

Remember, this step does not assure final and successful implementation. An action goal must be followed by development of a plan to achieve that goal, so think of translating a future vision into action as having two steps: developing a goal from the vision as discussed in this chapter, and developing an action plan, which is discussed in the next chapter.

9

STEP 7: Plan for Action

If we are to construct our own future, then we have to decide whether to intentionally involve ourselves in the exciting and creative act of creating it; we have to decide how to participate.

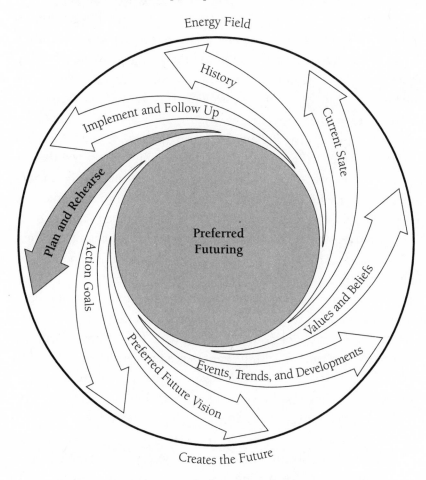

Steps to generate the energy field that manifests the future you want

Figure 9.1 Plan and Rehearse

Closing the Gap

The more clearly we articulate our desired future, the more conscious we become of the sizable gap between what we would like—our future vision and action goals—and the way things are now. This can become a source of frustration, guilt, or even depression. We can allow the frustration and depression to reduce our motivation and energy, which of course leads to more pain from continuing to live with the discrepancy. Or the frustration can become a push forward to do something.

But how can we take seriously the things that need to get done—how can we feel motivated and energetic and optimistic about closing the gap? There are two key strategies. First, engage in step-by-step structuring of the pathway to the future we want. Second, build in celebrations of small steps of progress along the way. Both these steps are incorporated into the Plan for Action.

In addition, as the Preferred Futuring process reaches the point where visions have been linked to tangible action goals and then to concrete action plans, fear and resistance to anticipated change or success may surface in the form of reduced motivation or involvement or increased negativity. It is typical and normal for people to question the validity and feasibility of new ideas, policies, regulations, procedures, and schedules. This questioning represents a natural and potentially constructive resource for those leading the Preferred Futuring process. In fact if there is no questioning, this may be symptomatic of an unhealthy situation in which inhibitions and fears keep people's questions and feelings underground. Dealing with ambivalence about the proposed actions and resulting changes is a critical element.

 TIP #7: View resistance as a resource; don't judge it negatively or see it as a block.

It is often valuable to take some time to acknowledge the voices in each of us that resist moving to action. This is a time to acknowledge the resistance as legitimate, to listen to the concerns and involve those inner voices in dialogue about how to address those concerns *and* still move toward the Preferred Future. Here are some typical comments that come from inside us and from other people:

- I wonder if this change will require our giving up some of our important traditions and values, which we worked hard to develop and hold very dear?
- I already feel overloaded: this just sounds like more time pressure and additional demands.
- What new gimmick are we going to have to learn?
- What kind of help are we going to get in making the shift?
- Are there really going to be improved payoffs for our clients, or for us?
- There may be some improvement, but I can see a couple of alternatives that I think would be better.
- I don't think they have thought it through. I can see some possible traps and side effects they haven't thought of.

The evidence is that these voices are a normal human response to change and represent one of the best resources to help avoid mistakes and locate bugs in the plan. Some of the best creativity for implementing change is in the heads and experience of the people who "resist" it. The question becomes, How can we harness resistance as a resource?

To constructively focus this negative energy and support success, and to close the gap between where we are and where we want to be, certain strategies are very useful. These strategies are incorporated into the three stages of the Plan for Action:

- *Phase 1:* Performing a Force Field Analysis
- *Phase 2:* Developing the First Steps in the Action Plan
- *Phase 3:* Rehearsing the First Steps of the Action Plan

The upcoming example illustrates Phases 1 and 2.

Example of Producing an Action Plan

An international manufacturer of automotive parts is concerned about lack of growth in its market share. One hundred members of the organization's top leadership are moving through the Preferred Futuring process. They have decided on their Preferred Future vision consisting of several priority images, and they have formed action planning teams around each one. As they face planning for action, they begin realizing that there may be resistance to these goals. Using Force Field Analysis to diagnose the situation helps develop sound strategies.

For example, one Preferred Future image is that in two years service to customers will have increased 20 percent in volume and quality with no increase in cost. As a result, the following goals have been developed: In two years, the organization will have: (1) increased the number of customers by 10 percent; (2) increased the level of services to current customers by 20 percent; and (3) improved the quality of service with no cost increase.

The team working on this priority brainstorms the forces driving and the forces restraining the movement to increased service to clients:

Driving Forces	Restraining Forces
Desire to serve more clients	Paperwork to process
Desire to decrease paperwork	Current skill level of workers
Efforts to increase skill level of workers	Tradition of steps in service contracts
Expectations of supervisors for improvement	Current level of supervision
	Worker irritation about no reward or recognition and about pushy supervisor

This picture of all the forces in play is an important tool for the group's strategic thinking, resulting in a better understanding of the situation. It helps them be more realistic about what they have to do. Before proceeding, it is important for each team to do a reality check by presenting their diagnosis to another team to see if they have forgotten anything and to ensure they are still on the right track.

The team then works on this problem of service to clients, developing the first steps in an Action Plan. To find ways to unfreeze the system and move it in the desired direction, this Action Plan must be based on: (1) reducing or removing one or more of the restraining forces, (2) changing a restraining force into a driving force, or (3) increasing the strength of one or more of the driving forces.

This strategy leads to two brainstorming sessions involving the team working on that goal. The first seeks ways to reduce, cope with, or transform restraining forces:

- Create a task force to reduce paperwork.
- Create an incentive for participation in training.
- Change attitudes of supervisors.
- Remove some supervisors.

The second seeks ways to activate, increase, and add to driving forces:

- Increase service motivation by collectively listing the payoffs of serving more clients.
- Have paperwork handled by fewer people.
- Computerize paperwork.
- Revise forms.
- Study techniques being used by other organizations to provide service.
- Upgrade service efficiency by having the most efficient workers become mentors.
- Provide targeted in-service training.

These ideas are briefly reviewed by the team, which then formulates a strategy that includes steps such as simplifying the forms and computerizing the system within six months, surveying customers to identify areas for improvement and best practices, and surveying employees for input about supervisors and best practices. Action teams responsible for supporting implementation are formed to deal with each of these tasks.

Primary Tools for Producing an Action Plan

As discussed earlier, translating an Action Goal into an Action Plan is a three-phase process.

Phase 1: Force Field Analysis

Why do some changes seem easy and some so hard or impossible to bring about? And how can we make change happen easier? In the 1940s Kurt Lewin, a social scientist studying individual and group behavior, developed a way to answer these questions.[1] He noticed that in any situation there were always "driving forces" pushing an individual or group toward change and other "restraining forces" simultaneously pushing to inhibit change. So, for example, changing conditions outside a group or even a department or whole organization might push for change, but the strength of group norms or cultural habit patterns might support continuing the old behaviors. If the push of opposing forces was equal, the result was no change. This state of equilibrium could be called a static state.

Force Field Analysis helps to identify strengths and resistances in the situation, and by providing clear guidance about the right actions, it makes change easier. Thus we can change the field that creates the current situation to create the future that we want. It can be that simple. But it usually is not, because we are unable to let go of old ways or perceived sources of power and control.

A Force Field Analysis involves the following procedure:

1. Make a force field chart for each action goal formulated in Step Six. The chart can be formatted like the one in the earlier example of driving and restraining forces, or you may use a more structured format like the one in Exhibit 9.1, listing the action goal and then outlining Supports and Resources and Restraints and Blocks in two separate dimensions with four categories:

EXHIBIT 9.1 FORCE FIELD WORKSHEET

Resources or Supporting Forces	Restraining or Blocking Forces

Forces inside me
or others

| Need for more people power felt by leaders | Reluctance of professionals to trust volunteers |
| More persons with a need to meaningfully connect with others outside work and feel they are making a difference, etc. | Lack of skill to recruit effectively, etc. |

Forces in groups or
between me and others

| Board decision to seek more volunteers, etc. | Conflict between staff and board about trusting volunteer to do important jobs |

Forces inside my organization
or current situation

| National trend to use volunteers more, etc. | Lack of budget for transporting volunteers, etc. |

Forces in the community,
national, or global situation

This is just a brief example. You will have many more forces in your diagnosis. Some forces will appear on both sides. You may not feel very sure about some and will need to get more facts.

It is usually helpful to share your force-field diagnosis with an-other team or colleague who knows your situation, to check your iden-tification of forces and to get ideas about additional forces you haven't considered. The more complete your assessment of the force-field sit-uation, the better the changes of successful action.

Source: Adapted from *Choosing the Future You Prefer,* E. Lindaman and R. Lippitt, 1979, Human Resource Development Associates, Inc., Ann Arbor, Michigan.

2. For their particular action goal, the planning teams brainstorm to identify the Supports and Resources and the Restraints, Blocks, Barriers within each of the four categories.

3. The teams mark with an asterisk (*) the most important items within each category and each column.

4. After prioritizing the forces, each team gets together with another team to share force fields and get additional suggestions.

5. The team then reconvenes and agrees on the most important forces, using criteria such as, If we reduce this force (or support this resource):

- Will it give us a quick or easy win (that is, help us reach our goal)?
- Will it be key to success?
- Is it doable?
- Can we get the resources to do it?

These will guide the work in Phase 2 below.

Phase 2: First Step Action Planning

Phase 2 determines who does what and when. It produces concrete, practical actions that begin movement toward implementing the Action Goal.

In First Step Action Planning, participants complete an Action Planning Worksheet for each Action Goal. Participants work as a team. And in completing the worksheet they should consider whether one or more people not in their team needs to be involved as key resources or implementers; if so, bring them into the process. An example of an Activity Planning Worksheet appears in Exhibit 9.2 (see page 90).

Parts d. and e. in the Activity Planning Worksheet involve milestones and celebration. Before having participants complete the worksheet, give them the following explanatory instructions:

1. To identify some milestones of progress toward your goal, it may be helpful to create a time line from now until the date when the final goal is reached. That is, set up a chart where you can keep track of the project as it develops, along the lines of this sample:

Now	T1		T2		T3		Goal
	Evidence		*Evidence*		*Evidence*		*Date*
	_____		_____		_____		
	_____		_____		_____		
	_____		_____		_____		

Set up some steps toward progress. Think of them as stepping stones toward the goal. Answer the questions: How can we know we are making progress? When will we know?

2. Now decide on appropriate times to check on progress (T1, T2, and so on) and decide on what the specific evidence of progress should be. Also consider what kind of data you will need to collect to get your evidence. How will you get the data? Who is responsible for the checking, or convening, or whatever is required for reviewing progress?

3. Have a celebration for each milestone. Don't wait until the end. The experience of shared celebration keeps energy and motivation high. Devote a brainstorming session to identifying ways to celebrate. This may seem like a strange activity, but let yourselves go and really have fun. Some examples might be:

- Report success to our supervisor
- Put it in the newsletter
- End the day with wine and cheese
- Think about next steps
- Hold a brainstorming session to share how we are feeling
- Take some time off

4. Look over your list of ways to celebrate. Which ideas appeal most to you? Who will take any needed "celebration leadership" or be responsible for preparation?

5. Later, if you haven't made the progress you hoped for, but you can discover why and can plan for correction or new direction, then this deserves celebration.

EXHIBIT 9.2 ACTION PLANNING WORKSHEET

a. To deal with the *barriers and resistance,* some first steps of action are:
   What Action?   *Who Does It?*

b. To involve and mobilize *resources for support and approval,* some
   steps of action are:
   What Action?   *Who Does It?*

c. To get started, who within our organization will take leadership?
   Who will do what? When will they do it?

d. What would be some first evidences of progress toward the goal—
   a milestone? What kind of data would be needed to determine
   achievement of milestone?

e. How might we celebrate upon reaching a milestone? What would
   be a meaningful reward?

f. Right now you deserve congratulations and a celebration for completing this first draft of a planning design. What will you do?

After completing the worksheet, participants have a set of concrete first steps toward their end goal, and some milestones with which to judge progress.

Phase 3: First Step Rehearsal Agenda

Good intentions do not guarantee success. Rehearsing the first steps of the Action Plan greatly increases the likelihood of specific implementation success. For example, if the Preferred Futuring meeting has involved a group of civic leaders and one of their Action Goals is "We want a safer downtown," a first step in their Action Plan may be to see the mayor and present their ideas. Those civic leaders who will actually see the mayor, anticipating a positive or negative response, may find it useful to role-play the meeting so as to anticipate the mayor's response and thus make a better presentation.

Many times people will tell us that although they resisted taking time to role-play and rehearse their conversation with individuals or teams, it was very helpful.

Ideally the rehearsal occurs during the Preferred Futuring meeting, immediately after the First Step Action Plan has been developed. It can, however, occur after the meeting. The format for the First Step Rehearsal can follow that of a play. That is, the group forms a practice trio (consisting of the people who will be taking the action) and finds a comfortable space to interact without being too close to another trio.

Decide who is going to be the first Practitioner.

The Practitioner selects and announces an opinion, attitude, or confrontation he or she wants to practice dealing with, for example, visiting the mayor.

Practitioner selects one of the two trio-mates or gets one to volunteer to take the role of the Confronter, for example, the mayor.

The third person will have the important dual jobs of Observer and Facilitator.

Practitioner briefs Confronter as to the situation in which the interaction will take place and who the Confronter is in the real situation (that is, what job or role, what relationship to Practitioner, what general attitudes to have). Not too much detail is provided, just enough to give the person the feel of the role.

Act I. The Observer starts the action. (That is, "Okay, it's 10 A.M. in their office. You are just walking in to try to get involvement.")

The Observer watches the interaction. How does Practitioner respond to the confrontation? What is the effect on Confronter? In what direction is the interaction going?

Intermission. Observer cuts the action after five to seven minutes, as soon as it is obvious how things are going.

Observer leads a five- to ten-minute discussion, asking Practitioner how he or she felt the interaction was going, asking Confronter how he or she felt about being in the role, and what was learned. Then Observer shares his or her own observations.

Next, Observer leads the trio in a brainstorming session on alternative strategies or approaches. Practitioner jots these suggestions down as preparation for a retry.

Now Practitioner reflects on the different ideas and decides which one, or combination, to try.

Act II. Observer starts the action as before and lets the new try unfold.

Intermission. Observer cuts again action after five minutes and leads a discussion of what happened with the changes from the first try?

Acts III, IV, and so on. (Optional, depending on time.) Practitioner may decide on a second try, or ask to observe one of the two others handling it, because they seem to have an interesting idea.

Next Encounter. Now rotate roles. Second Practitioner announces which confrontation he or she wants to practice coping with. The sequence is now repeated.

Critical Review. Finish the practice session by summarizing:

- What principles of successful action were discussed or otherwise clarified?
- What traps to successful action were identified?

These findings can be reported out to the team.

In the First Step Rehearsal, it must be clear that we are not playing for keeps in these situations, and there are no mistakes. These activities can provide supportive feedback with a chance to repeat the practice and give feedback to the overall implementation plans.

Completion of the First Step Rehearsal completes Step Seven in the Preferred Futuring process. The next step is implementing the plan, but before we turn to that it will be useful to assemble a few more tools.

Enhancement Tools for Producing Action Plans

There is an optional tool that can help you identify and acknowledge supports and resistances to goals and thus help develop more effective action plans: Strategy Development.

In addition, the Internal Dialogue tool deals with resistance within participants as action steps are taken.

Strategy Development

To foster innovative, out-of-the-box thinking, consider using this optional Strategy Development activity. It is done after the Force Field Diagnosis (Phase 1) and before the Phase 2 First Step Action Planning.

This activity has the following procedure.

1. After the Phase 1 Force Field Analysis, select two to four of the most important Supports or Resources and Restraints or Blocks and do two brainstorming sessions:

- *Session 1:* All the ways to use key resources and supports
- *Session 2:* All the ways to remove, cope with, change key restraints or blocks

2. Review the brainstorming lists and discuss what two or three actions seem most important, doable, or strategic for achieving the desired outcomes.

This should produce a rich pool of ideas for implementing an Action Goal, and several places to begin. Consider this a warm-up activity for the First Step Action Planning activity.

Internal Dialogue and Support

The Internal Dialogue and Support tool is an option for helping participants acknowledge resistance inside themselves. It is a way of listening to and learning from our internal voices—the voices supporting the risks, commitments, and new investments of energy associated with the planned changes, and the voices supporting caution and a conservative approach to initiating change. It can be used either during or after the Rehearsal.

The procedure is as follows:

1. Format a "Quotes Overheard" Worksheet, which involves dividing a flip chart page into quadrants that represent (1) the internal voices of support, (2) the individuals and groups that reinforce these voices of support, (3) the internal voices of caution, and (4) the individuals and groups that reinforce these voices of caution. See Exhibit 9.3.

2. Fill in the worksheet.

3. You have now identified some persons and groups whom you perceive as supportive of your plans for action, and also some non-supporters. There are usually several things we need to do and can do to develop supports. Spend a few minutes on some start-up thinking about the following points:

a. Clarify what support we would like and can use. For example, we may need administrator approval, help from some co-worker or department, a critical review of ideas from others, access to key persons and resources from others.

b. Briefly and clearly present your needs for help to those supporting you.

EXHIBIT 9.3 INTERNAL DIALOGUE AND SUPPORT WORKSHEET

Internal Voices of Support, Enthusiasm	Internal Voices of Caution, Self-Protection
External Supports for These Voices (Persons, Groups)	External Supports for These Voices (Persons, Groups)

c. Recruit, sell, or otherwise involve those who are important to you but not part of your current support system, that is, who are currently neutral.

d. Pay special attention to any nonsupporters and critics, and devise specific plans to add them to your support, or at least acceptance, system.

This Internal Dialogue is done by each individual—a silent inquiry—then shared in planning teams, and the information used to improve your First Step Action Plans.

TIPS FOR CREATING AN ACTION PLAN

To increase the chances for successful implementation of the Action Plan, create the plan using the following perspective and some of the following tools.

1. Be willing to listen, consult, clarify, and accept. Rather than being defensive, demonstrate the skills of objectivity with an interest in learning and clarifying. A listening and probing posture may reveal areas of misinformation. It can also reveal very practical data useful for skilled and intelligent Action Plans. To the degree that people are being consulted and listened to, they are more likely to be open to new ideas and different points of view about proposed changes.

2. Be ready to validate ideas and demonstrate feasibility. Counsel the groups that are translating priorities into action about the importance of linking recommendations to research or a knowledge base of some kind, as a way of demonstrating feasibility. It can be very helpful to arrange visits of participants to demonstrations where the proposed strategy is already being used, or to bring resource people to share their relevant success experiences.

3. Involve people in revising and enriching the plan. The use of a first-draft plan for action that is available for revision and discussion is a good way to involve larger numbers of people who were for some reason left out of the process earlier. It is possible to hold discussions to suggest improvements and revisions. To involve people and improve the quality of the action effort, have people brainstorm all the ideas they can list about effective implementation or all the ways the effort might be hindered.

4. Use rehearsal and practice opportunities to reduce the risk of failure or anxiety about new competencies required by any changes. This can be very helpful in providing opportunities to discover what it will be like and rehearse ways of coping with new tasks and expectations.

Conclusion

Now that you have an Action Plan to achieve your goals, the next chapter suggests several ways to create a structure for the successful implementation of that plan.

10

STEP 8: Create a Structure for Implementing the Plan

Sometimes it is easier to be a result of the past—than a cause of the future.
—Ashlei Brilliant

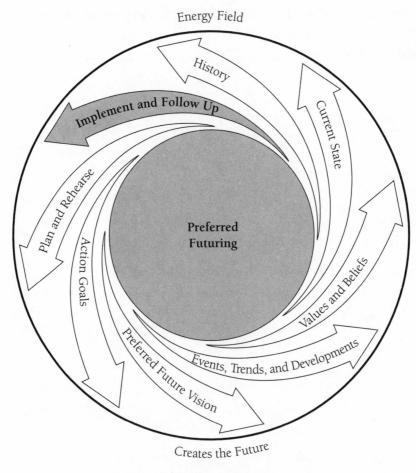

Steps to generate the energy field that manifests the future you want

Figure 10.1 Implement and Follow Up

Acting for Change

As an Action Plan begins to be implemented and achieve initial success, it is easy to lose focus. Other challenges occur, and there is a very real danger that the organization will slip back into old habits unless the new behaviors, processes, and level of operation are supported and reinforced.

As we have helped people create and sustain change in their systems over the years, we have noticed two basic postures toward planning and future thinking. In the *reactive posture,* people feel they lack personal or collective potency to initiate action successfully. They are most often ready to respond negatively to plans and expectations of others, and often exhibit a fatalistic attitude, assuming that "what will happen will happen." In the *proactive posture,* people feel they have the power to develop and initiate their own plans and exercise their freedom to respond to their own needs and ideas for action. They are most often ready to confront efforts of others to control their actions and plans. They have developed the ability to generate and initiate active images of desired outcomes.

Either of these two postures can be manifest at any level of organizational systems that we have worked with. These two different orientations toward past experience and future action significantly influence the way any of us project ourselves into the future as individuals, teams, or entire organizations.

As change agents (managers, leaders, trainer-developers), our great challenge is to reinforce in others a "forward thinking" attitude. And we must contribute to collective imaginative excursions into desired futures, in a context of thinking and acting in a whole-systems manner. This can be facilitated by creating a structure to monitor and support the proposed changes, a structure that helps institutionalize the new results or processes. Creating such a structure is, however, one of the most neglected parts of many change processes.

 TIP #8: Follow-up support and celebration can determine daily and long-term success or failure.

Successful implementation of the Action Plan often depends on how strongly leadership as well as others commit to the long-haul support of the effort, and how well we have built a monitoring and support structure. But this leadership involvement and structure can take many different forms, as the following brief examples indicate.

• In a city where Preferred Futuring was done, a small office with paid staff who handled the administrative follow-through activities was the major vehicle for support and follow-up. They were linked to a small team of volunteers and key leaders who kept a finger on the pulse of the effort and provided active support and coaching. They were also linked to the consultants (who had helped them design the process) for coaching or advice as needed.

• In a medium-sized private hospital, monitoring the implementation process was done by a cross-functional team with representatives from several layers of the system. Working closely with the training and development department and the executive leadership team, they identified and initiated activities such as coaching or training or realignment of responsibilities that supported the changes.

• In a manufacturing organization, the executive leadership team followed through on the monitoring responsibility. They reported out to their larger management team and solicited help for needed action as was indicated. This continually communicated the state of the implementation effort. The executive team also involved key people in support activities on an as-needed basis.

• In a very large utility company that had initiated a redesign process, the internal organization development consultant contracted with top leadership for the resources she would need; she guaranteed saving them twenty-five million dollars within five years in exchange for the resources. She contracted with each division leader she and her team worked with to track savings based on their redesign work; each piece of work had to have business results to be worth doing. The criteria and processes differed from division to division, but she was able to deliver the savings in four years rather than five!

To create a structure for implementing the Action Plan—for institutionalizing it—the available tools fall into three general categories:

- Assessing and Documenting Progress
- Spreading the Action Plan Through the System
- Supporting the Work Teams

Tools for Assessing and Documenting Progress

I think assessing and documenting progress (successes and learnings) is one of the most overlooked activities, and one that can have high payoff for relatively little investment in any change effort. One example shows the value of documentation.

During the first year of a school improvement effort that was using futuring, nine of twenty-three schools in an urban district volunteered to be in the project's first phase. Each school building had a "change team," and one member from each change team was specially trained during a half-day session as a documenter. These documenters collected standardized observations that tracked the teams' activities and noteworthy impacts on teacher and student involvement, innovative teaching activities, and attitudinal climate. The documenters used a questionnaire to assess and diagnose the climate in the organization and establish a baseline against which to measure improvement.

The information helped assess progress and initiate midcourse adjustments. At a significant milestone, the information was disseminated and used to recognize and celebrate success and to recruit increased involvement for the second phase of the change process. Over half the first-year change team participants were so proud and excited about their successes and professional growth that they volunteered to help other schools that wanted to become involved.

In supporting change and institutionalizing it, a major factor is gaining satisfaction and gratification from evidences of success. And so documenting success is critical. In creating an assessment and documentation structure, consider the role of the documenter.

The Role of the Documenter and the Skills Required

Even though the documenter role is one of the most important in the change effort, it is the most unrewarded and overlooked of all the roles on a project or program team. To build status and motivation, it helps to provide training in the necessary skills—and time for learning and practicing the role. It also helps to provide opportunities for progress reporting, such as newsletters, management meetings, staff review sessions, and annual reports. The main point: the documenter is a very important member of the team and does much for both the internal functioning and the external relations of your project or pilot program; the role is a steering tool, a learning tool, and a public relations tool.

How many documenters there are and who is selected varies according to the situation. In the previous example, each school building had a change team and each team had a documenter. In a large business, each department might have a documenter. In a small business, one of the leaders of the planned change might be the documenter. In selecting a documenter, keep in mind that you need someone with the observation and communications skills to effectively document the nature of the progress or lack of progress, provide data for reports to management, provide support material for qualitative or quantitative evaluation, and provide data for planning next steps.

Key tips for documentation:

1. Have a clear understanding of the purpose of the documentation—to evaluate successes, to guide next steps, and to provide data for progress reports and evaluation.

2. Use headlines to organize copious notes of data.

3. Document information about process (how things were done) as well as content (topics or issues discussed) at meetings.

4. Provide anecdotal richness along with condensed objective summaries.

5. Have a common outline for documenters to follow in writing up events.

6. Keep notes chronologically, using a new folder for each month.

7. If you have more than one documenter in an area, divide up the job so that no one feels overloaded.

8. Use notes to orient new participants or to brief the media.

9. Get good at co-authorship.

10. Don't be shy, self-conscious, or apologetic about keeping notes and asking for help.

In creating the documenter role, it is also helpful to provide some assessment and documentation tools, such as Documenting a Successful Practice and the Reality Checklist.

Documenting a Successful Practice

How does a documenter document? In the school example cited earlier, the innovative practices of individual teachers were documented by interviewing teachers about their classroom activities that worked. This documentation was then distributed to other teachers. This same form of documentation could be used for any aspect of the planned change effort, such as methods for dealing with resistance and stress or other techniques and processes.

In documenting a practice, I suggest keeping the description of the practice to one sheet, or two at most, and following the interview outline in Exhibit 10.1.

In documenting a practice, also keep in mind the following tips:

- Make sure that you can duplicate and disseminate documented practices. And invoke a deadline for submission and production.

- Develop a process for screening practices, so that you can decide on the most valuable practices to follow up on with the inventor.

- Make sure practices are documented in a uniform format, are readable and user-friendly, even bound attractively.

The Reality Checklist

Another way of documenting progress so as to make midcourse corrections and celebrate successes is to take the pulse of the people being affected by the change process—all the stakeholders. This pulse taking can be done by the documenter or by the leader of the change effort. I recommend that it be done periodically, the first time being very soon after the Action Plan has been developed and implementation has begun.

In Appendix A, there is a sample of what I call a Reality Checklist. This example is larger than the typical checklist because I have tried to include most of the questions we have found useful over the years. Respondents fill out the Reality Checklist anonymously, with the only instruction given to them being to move quickly and mark the first reaction that comes to mind. The data are summarized and used by the change team to monitor progress and current attitudes and to take corrective action or continue current actions based on the data. The data also need to be shared with the whole system to create a common understanding of current progress and any corrective action that needs to be taken.

EXHIBIT 10.1 INTERVIEW OUTLINE WORKSHEET

Interview Outline

1. What name or title would you give the practice?

2. What will the practice accomplish?

3. What does the practice look like in action (verbal snapshots of step-by-step action)?

4. What are the major payoffs (such as reduced costs, reduced errors, improved customer satisfaction, learnings and growth, and so on)?

5. What are the traps to avoid in using this practice?

6. What are the most important skills, materials, budget, or whatever to make this practice work?

7. Are there any variations on the practice that have been tried or could be recommended?

8. What is the name of the inventor of the practice?

9. How can one get in touch with the inventor for further follow-up? (List address and phone number if possible.)

Tools for Spreading the Action Plan Through the System

The Action Plan created in Step Seven is a product of a meeting or series of meetings usually attended by part of the organization or system—a significant part, perhaps, but still only part. (In some cases it can be the whole organization.) To increase the chance that the Action Plan will achieve the Action Goals and Preferred Future, other parts of the organization or system must be involved in the process.

To spread the Action Plan through the organization or system, you can use one of the following tools or create your own:

- Cascading Down the Action Plan
- Spreading Success
- Ingraining Preferred Futuring into the System

Cascading Down the Action Plan

If the entire organization did not go through the first seven steps of the Preferred Futuring process, the Action Plan can be *cascaded down* the lower levels of the organization. Let me illustrate.

After a well-known food chain CEO and his management team finished a three-day Preferred Futuring event for strategic planning, they had alignment with a common vision, a new mission with guiding principles, and action plans to move the company in the right direction. These plans included a way to involve the total corporate staff in actively shaping as well as supporting the mission and vision.

The internal human resources director and each VP replicated the strategic planning process with the department leadership staff. The staff was presented with the Preferred Future Visions and Action Goals, and they then fleshed these out with more operational detail and made some changes. This yielded a review and understanding of the mission; development of departmental visions, missions, and action steps aligned with the company mission; and managers who understood the process for use with their staffs.

The human resources staff then helped the managers implement the visioning process in each department with the remaining supervisors and work teams. The result was a whole organization aligned with and supportive of the company mission, an organization that also had a clear view of how it would actively support and implement that mission.

This process also began to be applied in project teams as well. Projects began starting off by reviewing how they were formed, envisioning success, identifying blocks and supports, then developing their action plans and rehearsing for success.

Spreading Success

Another way to spread the Action Plan, similar to the cascade-down activity, is to foster the spread of successes.

For example, as one result of a Preferred Futuring process, a community initiated a citizens' council and found that this spread to several neighboring communities. Because of this, and actively celebrating this fact, the practice became esteemed in the first community. This reduced some of the resistance to continuing the citizen council.

Often change in one part of a system can be viewed with suspicion by other parts of the system. This can contribute to increased resistance to the change process. It is thus often necessary to make a conscious effort to help people learn about the innovation while not losing face. In one case a chief engineer had led his management team and thousand-person organization through the process of developing a vision and mission of excellence for their operation. He surveyed the needs of his internal customers (marketing, manufacturing engineering, materials management, and finance) and determined areas of weakness and necessary steps to achieve excellence in his operation. This allowed him to report back to his "partner-customers" about their feedback and what he was going to do about it.

When he reported this process and data to his boss, it had such a high impact that it gained his boss's support. His maverick efforts became further legitimized when his peers wanted to learn more about what he was doing to garner such support. This led to other parts of the system more deeply understanding the changes his part of the system was making to better interface with them. It built good will and support, and it helped those other parts of the system to begin to look into their own operations as a part of the whole system. It also increased the team's motivation to continue developing this process and resist the temptation to revert to older, less effective methods as quality and productivity pressures rose.

Ingraining Preferred Futuring into the System

When the Preferred Futuring and Action Planning process has led to initiating successful change efforts, there can be a tendency to relax and say, "Whew, that's done." This can be a mistake. The Preferred Futuring process is an effective tool to continuously stay proactive and effectively manage change. Here are some ideas that have worked:

• *Continuous scanning for events, developments, and trends.* Once people understand the value of ED&T scanning, it is easy to establish an ongoing ED&T scanning function. This can help anticipate developments in the marketplace or within the organization, and help revise the vision and plans proactively along the way.

Some companies have an ED&T scanning function that feeds information to the few people responsible for strategic planning. This is usually ineffective, because the information becomes unavailable to everyone who needs it to develop a collective vision of the desired future. As discussed in Chapter Six, ED&T data must be broad-based and shared widely.

• *Internal cadre development.* To get involvement in change and manage that change, internal teams can easily be trained to involve their units in Preferred Futuring. It is critical though that these teams be given on-site consultation and support. In one organization we saw this support take the form of a yearly progress evaluation process. The cadre began to actively take responsibility for the continued training and support of others and spreading innovations across departments. It also helped spread the use of Preferred Futuring in problem solving groups and among supervisors.

- *Futuring as part of the yearly business planning process.* Linking mission, goals, and annual business planning requirements to daily activities is often a challenge. A large engineering organization had always seen completion of the annual business plan as an irrelevant chore required by corporate, having nothing to do with what actually happened. It had used Preferred Futuring to achieve alignment with a mission and detailed Preferred Futuring vision and action plans to close the gap between its current state and vision of excellence. It revised its internal planning processes so that a yearly review of the vision and the previous year's accomplishments, followed by establishment of new action plans with attached budget requirements, became the annual business planning process. This produced the required business plan, institutionalized the futuring process, gave meaning to the annual business planning process, and reduced redundant activities.

- *Yearly re-visioning for continuity.* To kick off the year's initiatives, such as improvement processes and so on, each year can start with a review of the old vision by the entire staff. This helps build the team, provides a powerful orientation event, gets new and old personnel involved quickly, and—most important—provides continuity.

In a system where there had been a recent high retirement rate, this provided an opportunity for building the new team. It also provided an opportunity to organize around the new resources represented by new members of the staff, while retaining a sense of continuity.

- *Rehearsal and support.* When implementation actions are taken, the risks feel real, and it is important to plan for at-the-elbow support. In some situations this may mean the opportunity for a telephone conversation or a debriefing meeting immediately after the first try-out of new processes or activities. It may also involve support from working with a peer; the use of teamed pairs in the context of a larger group is one of the most meaningful bases of support when there is a chance to debrief and review and improve. Frequently, teaming like this is seen as not cost-effective, but the added value is usually worth it.

Tools for Supporting Effective Team Processes

A great deal has already been written about developing and supporting effective teamwork during the change process. So I will share only a few ideas that people have found very helpful:

- The Team Process Review Sheet
- The Task Force Summary Report
- Ways to Optimize Team Productivity

Team Process Review Sheet

At any point in the implementation process, teams can ask themselves how well their members are working together. Each team member is asked to step aside for a moment and become an observer of the group and the way the member and the group have been performing on this task. There are three questions each team member should answer:

1. What are some evidences of an effective team that I have seen?
2. What are some evidences of weaknesses and needs for improvement in the ways we are working?
3. What are some things that I as a member could do to improve team productivity?

After answering the questions, the team members should be directed to take ten minutes to *quickly* share their responses to each question. Everyone shares #1 responses, then #2 responses, and then #3 responses. There should be no discussion; everyone just listens to each other. After that, they take a look at the ideas for improvement that surfaced (not any other comments that may have been made). If there is a consensus on an idea, they should agree to implement it as they go back to their regular work.

Task Force Summary Report

When temporary groups are formed, a helpful organizational tool is the Task Force Summary Report. Appendix B provides a sample of this report.

Ways to Optimize Team Productivity

To optimize team productivity when implementing the Action Plan, here is a brief description of what I think are the most important guidelines.

The first guideline involves the optimal size for teams. A variety of researchers on group dynamics and participation find that a group of twelve is optimal. Interaction and participation studies reveal that in groups larger than this, some members stay hidden and don't participate; conversely, in very small groups certain resources are missing. This seems to be a good guideline for task forces, steering committees, and operating committees.

But there are a variety of group tasks for which different sizes of groups are particularly relevant. Here are some of our observations and conclusions.

- *The two-person group:* There are many tasks where individuals need the reinforcement of a partner in order to carry through on commitments to themselves or others, for example, to do some special task with set dates to share and report to each other. The buddy system is a very basic unit for support, planning, or action. Also we have found that co-leadership greatly increases the quality of leadership of teams, committees, task forces, and training groups.
- *The three-person group:* This group is very important for skill practice. Most role-playing or reality-skills practice designs (like the First Step Rehearsal discussed in Chapter Nine) call for a practitioner, a protagonist, and an observer and feedback specialist to provide data for subsequent rounds of practice. The objective is to give everyone a chance to practice and practice again after feedback. Three is the critical number to maximize practice time for each person and still have a feedback resource. The trio is also excellent for peer consultation where each person is planning implementation activities and using the others as consultants.
- *The five-to-seven-person group:* This is an excellent size for special task forces. Each member gets more air time than in a twelve-person group, and they can more quickly get a task done.

As mentioned earlier, groups with fewer than twelve may mean reduced resources, so smaller task force groups should be formed so that adequate resources and diverse perspectives are assured.

The second guideline involves some proven methods for improving team productivity.

In workshops and consultations aimed at improving the productivity and level of cooperation of task forces and project teams, the following activities have been evaluated as successful:

- In consultation with other team members, take time to design a meeting process that supports the agenda (use the DPPE Model discussed in Chapter Twelve).
- Develop feedback and evaluation tools for improving cooperation and work efficiency.
- Design meetings at which team goals are set so that consensus, commitment, and stepwise planning are achieved.
- Develop a stop-action tool to use when meetings seem to bog down.
- Help teams develop a self-evaluation check sheet for assessing evidences of quality of work.
- Hold skill practice sessions for leaders in handling critical issues that come up in their leadership of a team.
- Develop a reward and recognition procedure for team achievements.

Conclusion

I strongly recommend that you consider the activities discussed in this chapter—and create a structure for implementing the Action Plan. Avoid the trap of leaving the Preferred Futuring session and letting the system slide back into old behaviors and habits. Why evoke the power of the Preferred Futuring process and not give yourself an even higher probability of success?

Using the Preferred Futuring Model

Part Three shows how to use the tools presented in Part Two. Chapters Eleven through Thirteen walk you through the entire Preferred Futuring process for different types of organizations and systems. Then Chapter Fourteen shows how to know when to use Preferred Futuring, and Chapter Fifteen shows specific applications.

11

Putting Preferred Futuring into Practice: The Basics

Everything that is possible now was at one time impossible. When we look forward with hope and expectation, it is an act of creating that empowers and creates the present we want. So we must learn to speak out and say, "Yes, this is where we prefer to go."

Some Start-Up Issues

My purpose now is to give a more detailed picture and feeling for how you put together the eight steps of the Preferred Futuring model. This should help you use the model yourself.

Almost all organizations and institutions go through the Preferred Futuring process in much the same way, following the track outlined in Chapter Twelve. Communities go through on a significantly different track, discussed in Chapter Thirteen. Regardless of which track you follow, however, before you even begin designing the process it is worthwhile to think about some common start-up issues: creating the right mood within the organization and dealing with resistance.

Beginning to Think in Future Tense

To move an organization into a mood in which it will be more receptive to Preferred Futuring, it helps to begin thinking in the future tense.

And this in turn requires several changes in our usual perspective—more particularly, changes in how leaders think.

First, in the past most organizations entrusted the responsibility for planning to a small planning group or leadership team at the top; goal setting and planning were assumed to be the responsibility of top leadership. Preferred Futuring, in contrast, is based on the conviction that people at every level of the organization must be involved in the planning process—that is, if implementation of the change is to be focused on the right things and be successful.

Closely related to this is the belief that data for significant future thinking are in the heads of stakeholders at all levels. Several years ago, I heard a story about the president of a Japanese ship-building company. He said his firm was much more productive than other shipyards partly because of the fifteen hundred ideas that had come up the prior year from the workers. All these ideas were actively appreciated and acknowledged, and many of them improved company productivity and indicated new directions and actions.

Another story confirming that same opinion came from an internal consultant in a high-tech American firm that had successfully reduced the cost of its product. The firm was able to maintain high quality at a much lower cost and beat the Japanese competition because the consultant interviewed the workers in all parts of the production process and used their ideas—which were more significant, in total, than just the few ideas that came from the research department. The people on the line really knew what the possibilities were for improving the quality of the product.

Second, although the futuring process must have broad participation, leadership must sponsor the futuring process. This leadership may be in the form of a small homogeneous group at the top that takes ad hoc responsibility for leading the total program. Or it may be a heterogeneous group from all levels of the system that coordinates the process. Or a nomination procedure may be set up to identify key persons in all parts of the system who have visibility and influence or local respect. (This last approach is often used in large systems such as communities or large school districts, and will be discussed in Chapter Thirteen.)

Regardless of the form of leadership, it must coordinate the Preferred Futuring and planning activities and assess the feasibility of agreed-upon priorities. Why? When people at all levels are warmed up to creative thinking about future products or services and directions, this provides a tremendous variety and wealth of ideas. People are able to make serious judgments and come to consensus on preferred future scenarios. The ideas that emerge from lower levels of the organization will have a practicality and wisdom about implementation, yet may lack a more global perspective about competition, overall economic requirements, and so on. On the other hand, top leadership often has more global strategic perspectives that are valuable, yet lack specific implementation ideas. The responsibility of leadership is to make sure the diverse contributions are combined to maximize benefit to the whole organization.

Third, the organization must see the value of futuring. People must see that every organization or human system is in the process of continuous change and development, and so the issue is basic and the choice is crucial: whether to cope reactively with the future created by others, or to work innovatively and strategically to create our Preferred Future. The leadership team (a board, an executive leadership team, a group of city leaders) and decision makers in the system must want to make this shift within the system.

Dealing Successfully with Resistance

Among members of any group assembled to do Preferred Futuring, there can be multiple sources of resistance to taking responsibility for our own future—resistance to the idea that futuring really works. It can be useful, early in the futuring process, to acknowledge these, and either of the methods discussed in this section does this.

Brainstorming Prior Messages

Resistance can be acknowledged by brainstorming messages that we remember from our early socializers such as parents, teachers, and other older adults—people who shaped our attitudes and beliefs toward our power to initiate plans and actions to obtain what we want. A typical brainstorming list might look like this:

Messages That Discourage Futuring
Que Sera, Sera
Oh, be realistic
Beggars can't be choosers
You'll give your mother a heart attack
Are you telling me you are better than the rest?
Live for today
Be sensible
Get your head out of the clouds
You can't have everything
Keep your feet on the ground
Face reality
God has the plan
Why stick your neck out?

Messages That Encourage Futuring
Go for it
You would be good at it
Nothing ventured, nothing gained
May your dreams be reality
Try and try again
Learn from failures
Where there's a will there's a way
Problems are opportunities in disguise
Paint a star on the window to wish on during cloudy nights
The sky's the limit
If the world gives you lemons, make lemonade
Don't give up
Today's truth is tomorrow's limit
You have to have a dream to have a dream come true

This activity breaks the ice, helps us cope with hesitation, and prepares us to mobilize our imaginative intelligence and accept the importance of futuring.

Acknowledging Our Irrational Beliefs

Albert Ellis, founder of the school of rational therapy, spoke of disputing "irrational beliefs" as a way to heal ourselves.[1] I have borrowed from his thinking and created ten irrational beliefs that may produce resistance to Preferred Futuring:

1. I *must* have sincere love and approval almost all the time from all the people I hold significant.
2. I *must* prove myself thoroughly competent, adequate, and achieving at all times in all situations.
3. If things do not go the way I would like them to go, the results will be catastrophic, and I will not be able to deal with them.
4. There is something wrong with people who commit misdeeds toward me, and they need to be shown that they are wrong.
5. If something seems dangerous or fearsome, I must become terribly occupied with it or upset with it.
6. People and things should turn out better than they do and I have to view it as awful and horrible if I do not quickly find good solutions to life's hassles.
7. Emotional misery comes from external pressure and there is nothing I can do about my reaction to people and things that happen.
8. It is easier to avoid facing difficult situations and expressing my irritations than it is to take responsibility for expressing my irritations and for expressing myself and dealing with the situation and declaring what I want.
9. I am the person I am because I have always been this way and I always will be; there is nothing I can do about it.
10. If I am lucky, I will be happy; there is nothing I can do about it.

When we acknowledge these irrational beliefs, it empowers us to have the courage to choose our Preferred Future.

Some Words of Wisdom

As you use the Preferred Futuring process with any group or large system, please keep in mind a few lessons that I have learned over the years.

- *Do not limit planning activities for the whole organization to a small team.* This greatly limits the resources of imagination and experience mobilized for the effort, and it drastically reduces the level of commitment and motivation available for goal implementation.
- *Do not limit your scan of the environment for events, trends, and developments with implications for your possible futures.* While limiting your scan may be a response to the explosion of information in recent years, a better response is to organize this information so that it can be easily scanned and retrieved by individuals and teams from as many sources as possible, such as newspapers, TV, trade journals, newsletters, and so on.
- *Do not confuse predicting and preferring.* Predicting relies on trend data and expert analysis. When people are asked to state preferences, this leads to clarifying values and intentions. And it can lead to a deeper understanding that results in confronting old beliefs or policies and connecting to our real passions and desires.
- *Do not move directly from identifying priority images to specific Action Goals without first performing a Force Field Analysis.* There must be a strategic analysis of strengths and weaknesses or driving and restraining forces that affect the prospects for successful implementation. This is a major tool for anticipating resistance and planning for it.
- *Do not limit the right-brain creativity during the more disciplined and convergent process of planning for implementation.* It is often advisable to initiate real mind-stretching brainstorming sessions of alternative ways to achieve specific outcomes. This helps avoid the temptation to revert to the way we have always done things.

- *Once good action plans have been made, do not skip the essential step of rehearsal or other forms of skill training.* When there is a sense of urgency or an emotional high created by a new collective vision, it is easy to go ahead unprepared for success. Rehearsal and training assure skilled implementation that is more likely to succeed, and succeed more fully.

- *Remember that although the eight-step Preferred Futuring process may seem linear, there is a certain amount of interaction between and among these steps.* For example, participants who are translating their Preferred Future vision into Action Goals (Step Six) should feel free to reexamine conclusions generated in the Historical Review (Step One). Or as participants begin implementing their Action Plan, they should, if the situation dictates, go back and change the plan. In any case, you should revisit the Preferred Future Vision annually as part of your business planning cycle or in three to five years as part of your strategic planning process. Keep in mind that as we get closer to our Preferred Future, our vision of it may change somewhat based on new data and increased wisdom.

Conclusion

Since the beginning of time, we have tried to predict or control future events. Things have not changed, except that we are becoming more aware of how much we really participate in future events. Use of imagination, whether it be idle dreaming or conscious intention, is what propels each of us into the future.

In the past, future thinking was the province of the prophet— and more recently of the science fiction writer—but now we are beginning to realize it is within the domain of every thoughtful person. In order to shape a preferred future, we are learning that we need to hold in our minds an image of that which we really want. Also becoming more evident is our responsibility and our task to participate with our fellow human beings in collectively choosing the future we want, a future that will benefit life not only in our organizations and communities but on this planet.

12

Preferred Futuring in Action for Organizations and Institutions

How then can we decide best about our own future? We make the best decisions when we are in community, with others of shared interest.

A Road Map of the Preferred Futuring Process

As Figure 12.1 shows, the Preferred Futuring event for an organization or institution is preceded by the leadership's making a commitment to Preferred Futuring, and by a preparation phase at which the futuring event is designed and any other preparatory work is done. Then at the Preferred Futuring event, the group goes through the eight-step Preferred Futuring process. Next, as the Action Plan is implemented, structure is added in the form of support, follow-up, evaluation, and celebration. The shape of Figure 12.1—a cone expanding as it rises—illustrates more people becoming involved in the process as it proceeds, more human energy being mobilized, and the increasing whole-systems generative energy field.

Let me describe the basic Preparation phase and the people involved in it, and then illustrate both the Preparation phase and the Preferred Futuring model with an example.

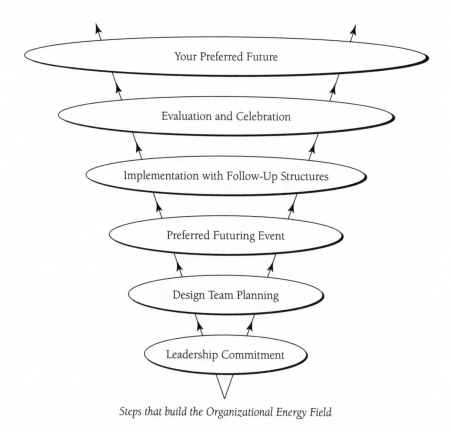

Steps that build the Organizational Energy Field

Figure 12.1 Preferred Futuring for Organizations and Institutions

The Preparation Phase

In all organizations and systems other than a community, preparation for the Preferred Futuring event is the responsibility of the microcosm design team.

This team will typically consist of fifteen to twenty stakeholders representing those who will attend the event from across the system, plus one or two facilitators who may be from inside or outside the organization.

The team provides necessary data on key issues and dynamics present in the system, develops a clear purpose and outcomes for the

Preferred Futuring event, and participates in developing the design for the two- or three-day event.

To be a microcosm, the team obviously must consist of people who represent different points of view within the whole system, including dissenting or minority viewpoints. As a result, because the team reflects the issues, fears, hopes, dreams, passions, and dynamics interacting within the whole organization, a very clear picture of the whole organization is produced, and produced in real time without having to go out and do traditional data gathering.

The primary tool used by the microcosm design team is the Data-Purpose-Plan-Evaluation (DPPE) Model.

The Data-Purpose-Plan-Evaluation Model

The DPPE Model is used at a series of meetings (usually two or three) of the microcosm design team, at which the Preferred Futuring event is planned. The DPPE Model provides a road map for the work of the team: collecting *Data* about the organization or the situation, setting a *Purpose* for the Preferred Futuring event, creating a *Plan* or agenda for the event, and *Evaluating* the results of the event.

Let me give a brief description of each part of the model—Data, Purpose, Plan, Evaluation—and then illustrate the model in the subsequent example. (As the design team goes through the model, it is directed by one of the leaders of the change effort or a small team of such people.)

* *Collecting data.* At the Preparation phase meetings, the design team identifies core diagnostic data about its system. Data can be assembled by having design team members educate each other about the key issues in the system. The purpose is to keep focused on the facts and get a finger on the pulse of the system.

At the first meeting, the design team members introduce themselves and tell what each does in the system. The task of the design team is outlined: participants are present as microcosmic representatives of the whole system, and it is imperative that they tell their truth about the world of the organization or the situation being discussed.

Then all the team members are asked to "tell their story"—their view of the situation—one at a time. Everyone is asked to listen to see and understand the world through the speaker's eyes. This helps the team move to thinking in whole-systems terms, and creates a deeper understanding and a common database within this microcosm team. Key data points of these stories are recorded on flip charts.

• *Setting the purpose.* Next, the team summarizes the data it has uncovered, notes the main themes, and develops a clear set of outcomes and a purpose for the Preferred Futuring event. This usually requires a lot of energy and discussion. The purpose of the Preferred Futuring event will be the touchstone that drives the Preparation phase. The team now has a clear focus and rationale for how activities will need to flow in the design phase. The purpose and outcomes also become a marketing statement that will draw people to the event.

• *Creating the plan.* The team agrees to a detailed plan for the meeting, including implementation steps leading up to the event; basically, the two- or three-day Preferred Futuring event is choreographed—what is going to happen and when, and who will participate in each piece of the agenda.

Throughout this step it is essential to check and see if the design team is still "on purpose." The design team knows what will and will not work with the large group and how to help that group move to deeper levels of risk in telling the truth about the way things are and need to be.

At this time the team finalizes who needs to be invited to the event.

• *Evaluating the results.* The team next develops ways to evaluate success during the Preferred Futuring event. There will be several design meetings before a plan is produced, and during this time, members of the design team are testing their ideas with their constituent stakeholders back in the system. At every design team meeting, there will also be evaluation of how the design team is working together.

During the Preferred Futuring event, the team collects data and, at the end of each day, reviews the data to determine if any redesign of the following day's agenda is necessary. A summary of the data is presented along with any agenda revisions at the start of days two and three. Thus the DPPE model adds to the growing common database at the Preferred Futuring event.

In addition, a logistics leader and small team need to be assembled and briefed. Their task is to manage and ensure smooth operation of all logistics during the event. This includes typing up and distributing information, ensuring work and instruction sheets are available at each table when needed, and other behind-the-scenes tasks.

Now let's see how all that you have read in this book comes together in real life.

An Example of the Preferred Future Process in an Organization

My consulting firm had been called in by the CEO of a hospital because he saw his leadership team—fourteen vice presidents and a medical director—as unable to make decisions and work in unison for a common cause. Even when decisions were apparently made, they often were never carried out.

Once we helped them come together as a team and align to a common mission and vision that captured their passion and commitment, they were about to make the common mistake of creating a mission and vision and then rolling it down the organization with a traditional top-down, one-way communication process. But by thinking of the whole system, they realized that without the rest of the system involved, their roll-down strategy would not engage the hearts and minds of the other key stakeholders and implementers, nor tap their resources to improve the mission.

They agreed to participate in a large-scale Preferred Futuring event, and they committed to participate in and support follow-up efforts. The event would include over a hundred participants from all levels of management, down to and including some key supervisors.

As a first step, we worked with the key internal organization development resource person to set up a Microcosm Design Team and help that team use the Data-Purpose-Plan-Evaluation Model.

Collecting Data

Over three days the design team, with our help, worked its way through the DPPE process, asking, "What do we now know about the people and the system?" A summary of the Data Collection part of the model looked like this:

- Hard working
- Angry, betrayed—not too late though, trust can be reestablished
- Highly educated
- Dedicated to system's success
- Not cutthroat or competitive
- Feel a member of the family
- More women than men
- Self-motivated
- Thirty to fifty years old
- Feeling overwhelmed
- Many long-term employees of over ten years
- Lack of trust in planning due to the past
- Leaders moved up in the ranks, no formal leader training
- Willing to give it one more shot
- Focused on daily survival
- Some teamwork between and within
- Feel fragmented
- Don't feel support from the top
- Corporate out of touch with issues out here
- Suspicion of this process
- Is corporate really behind this?
- Here we go again
- There is lack of follow-through in the system
- Leadership sends mixed messages

- Leadership complaints about each other weaken system and their image
- There is give-and-take in the system
- We need a process where we can ask real questions
- Is this just another exercise?
- We admire our leader and will follow him, but we don't know where he wants to go
- We need to hear a unified message

The team raised a number of concerns about follow-up. Members asked how the change process would be perpetuated if a financial crunch occurred, and how things would be kept from dying. They pointed out that teams working on strategic targets currently only included corporate officers, and they asked whether this would continue or whether the team would actually be integrated into this process. They wanted to know who was going to be accountable for follow-through. They also noted that it felt as though they were being asked to risk too much to "tell it the way it is" in front of the VPs.

These concerns were part of "their story," that is, the way they saw the situation. These core issues had to be dealt with at the Preferred Futuring event if the change efforts were to succeed.

Setting the Purpose

The microcosm design team agreed on a purpose and outcomes for the Preferred Futuring event, and provided additional rationale for the design and core issues to be clarified. Here's what they came up with:

Purpose:
To assure that corporate and department leaders share a common vision and that there is an enhanced sense of trust that we will work together to make our specific plan happen within a given time frame.

Outcomes:
1. Clarity about and acceptance of the mission statement
2. Input into and clarification of roles and responsibilities and a sense of empowerment to carry them out

3. Commitment to a plan to implement the mission
4. Evidence of corporate leadership's commitment to our plan
5. A stronger bond and sense of "team" in the whole system
6. A stronger network among the whole leadership team and getting to know each other better

As part of the Purpose step, the microcosm design team met with the executive leadership team to gain their agreement to the purpose, outcomes, and plan, and got their agreement to make the plan and commit to follow-up work. They got it all. The executive leadership team understood the process and what their role needed to be.

Creating the Plan

A sample Plan or agenda for the Preferred Futuring event is in Appendix C. (This agenda is only meant to be an example, not a rigid template for designing your futuring event.)

After the leadership team (all managers and supervisors) went through the Preferred Futuring process using the agenda in Appendix C, they replicated the Preferred Futuring steps in a series of staff meetings with their functional units. This included adding value to the mission and the action plan with more specific and relevant details from their areas.

In preparation for this second set of meetings, a half day of training in facilitation of these meetings and additional coaching was provided. A how-to manual was created for managers and another for supervisors to use in replicating the process throughout the system. This happened quickly in accordance with an agreed-upon time line.

Evaluating the Results

Within six weeks after the Preferred Futuring event, the results of these activities were communicated back to the executive team, which finalized the mission and vision based on this feedback. There was strong pride, celebration, and excitement as everyone accepted a mission and vision for their whole system that contained their passions and bore their fingerprints. The mission and vision did not go into a desk drawer to collect dust and guilt. They were used as living documents to guide daily operations and decisions in unit and cross-unit meetings.

The result was a new climate of trust and cooperation and operating as a whole system with much more collaborative and single focus. Innovations and cost savings began to appear in many areas. A year later the decision to implement Total Quality Management throughout the system was made. It took about 50 percent less time to accomplish this because the necessary structures and relationships had been created through the whole-systems Preferred Futuring change process. And because the organization had learned how to create a whole-systems change, installing Total Quality Management (the next whole-systems change) was easier, quicker, and cheaper than it would have been had they been starting from scratch.

Conclusion

Preferred Futuring is a very direct way to align a whole system with a new and exciting vision, recognize hidden resources and resistance, gain widespread employee participation, and create deep and rapid strategic change. This is always a very intense and focused time. What is most exciting is the way people's passions and creativity and deep yearnings are tapped and focused. As this happens from step to step in the Preferred Futuring process, the energy field for the desired future is rapidly built. Implementation and follow-up support maintain this generative field as it manifests as the new present for the whole system. It often feels to me that we are doing the soul work for the whole system and connecting at that level with everyone as one field of creative energy.

Let's see what this looks like in a different kind of human system—a community or city.

13

Preferred Futuring in Action for Communities

Our ability to project a collective Preferred Future ultimately defines our community and empowers us as a community.

A Different Approach for Communities

The last chapter discussed and illustrated the basic preparation for the Preferred Futuring event for organizations and institutions. Historically, Preferred Futuring had some of its earlier successes in the hands of its founders at city and state levels. So it is not surprising that it is such a powerful process for aligning and mobilizing human energy and resources at that level. More than any community development or planning process that I have seen, it generates enthusiasm, commitment, intent, whole-systems thinking, planning, cooperation, good will, and a focus on the right things. As one newspaper account stated, "While the process invites creativity and uninhibited thought, it has no room for prophecy, it feeds on reality and cultivates progress."[1]

Preferred Futuring, however, is used differently in communities than in organizations and institutions. In an organization or institution, typically the leader or the leadership team decides that the organization will benefit from the process and marshals the resources to make it happen. In communities, the process of preparation and going through the Preferred Futuring model is quite different; a consensus for going through the process must be built piece by piece, and the whole-system Preferred Futuring event is not a single meeting but several meetings over a period of time. How this happens is the subject of this chapter.

For communities, the process occurs in several phases:

- *Phase 1: The Future Sampler Meeting,* at which key community leaders decide whether Preferred Futuring is something they want to do.
- *Phase 2: The Start-Up Conference,* which is attended by block and neighborhood leaders. The Start-Up Conference spreads the Preferred Futuring process to the next level within the community.
- *Phase 3: Multiple Preferred Futuring Sessions* held throughout the community.
- *Phase 4: The Preferred Futures Scenarios Conference,* which can be attended by anyone in the community. At this conference the information from the community-wide futuring sessions is used to agree on the strategic priorities—that is, Action Goals, Action Steps, and responsibilities.

As Figure 13.1 shows, the Preferred Futuring process radiates out from a relatively small group of leaders, accumulating input from the entire community, before resulting in final Action Goals and an Action Plan at the Scenarios Conference. The process then continues as the Action Plan is implemented with paid and volunteer support, follow-up, and reviews. Citizen energy and participation are mobilized and increase over time.

Phase 1: The Future Sampler Meeting

The Future Sampler Meeting is typically convened by someone or a small group of people who want to create change; they become the meeting's leaders.

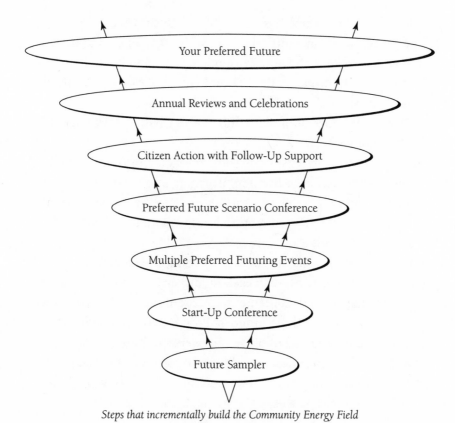

Steps that incrementally build the Community Energy Field

Figure 13.1 Preferred Futuring for Communities

The meeting helps a group of community leaders get a feel for Preferred Futuring and decide whether it should be a part of their planning process. The meeting takes participants (in an abbreviated manner) through a large part of the Preferred Futuring model discussed in Chapters Three through Ten, as you can see from reviewing the meeting's agenda:

1. Start the meeting with a statement of why we are here. Introduce the meeting leaders and explain what your responsibilities are. (Allow ten minutes for this.)

2. Check that everyone has signed in. State estimated length of meeting (from one-and-a-half to two hours, depending on what you have planned). (Allow five minutes.)

3. Introduce futuring—what it is and why it works. (Allow five to ten minutes.)

4. Review the rules of brainstorming from Chapter Three. (Allow five minutes.)

5. As a warm-up activity, share some relevant world, local, or community prediction or trend information, and encourage people to shout out ideas, *not to discuss them,* but rather to share the implications of the information for this particular community. (Allow ten minutes.)

6. Initiate a *Prouds and Sorries* activity about the community. Use table groups or trios, with each group having a sheet of paper for writing and a documenter to record input. Have each group mark their two or three proudest Prouds and sorriest Sorries after brainstorming. (Allow ten to twenty minutes.)

7. Call out these proudest Prouds and sorriest Sorries. Make a list of these on a flip chart in the front of the room. Have participants comment on themes and make other observations about this list. (Allow ten minutes.)

8. Prepare for future trip (see Chapter Seven). Present the Preferred Future task using key elements relevant to the group's specific situation. Be sure each table group has a flip chart and felt tip pen to write their future images. (Allow ten minutes.)

9. Have the table groups post their preferred images on the walls, and then have the whole group read them and vote, using the sticky-dot voting process discussed in Chapter Seven. (Allow ten to twenty minutes.)

10. Select the one item with the most votes, and then brainstorm the question, "What are all the things that might be done to move us toward that strategic outcome?" Record the suggestions on a flip chart at the front of room. Have a discussion about which ideas might represent innovative solutions or have a high potential for

success and what implementation might look like. (Allow ten to twenty minutes.)

11. Have table groups discuss for five minutes what it was like to do futuring and how it might be used, then report out and discuss in the larger group. This is the place to discuss and decide whether to use Preferred Futuring with the whole community, and if so, what the next steps are. (Allow fifteen to twenty minutes.)

12. End of session. Have participants read *Reaction* sentences and share the ones that best express their feelings. Reactions might include "This is just what we need; when do we start" or "Sounds too radical to me" or "This is worth considering and we should think about it." It may help to ask members to jot down their individual responses to these reactions first. It is also possible to hand out a written evaluation form. (Allow five minutes.)

13. State that volunteer help will be needed, and ask any who want to pitch in to sign a volunteer sheet at the door. These volunteers can help organize the Start-Up Conference described later in this chapter.

As a result of the Future Sampler Meeting, community leaders have enough information to make an informed decision. If they decide to use Preferred Futuring, the next step is to prepare for a Start-Up Conference. Another issue raised during or after the Future Sampler Meeting is formation of a documentation plan and team.

The Role of Documentation

A good documentation plan and team is a critical part of the Preferred Futuring effort for a community, and unfortunately, often one of the least-considered aspects. The documentation plan and team serve as a resource for:

- Media releases and other public education activities
- Orienting newcomers who want to become involved later

- Assessing progress toward goals
- Preparing reports to interested corporate, community, state, and national leaders
- Preparing requests for funding and information for annual reports
- Collecting media reports and other records that tell the story of the effort

The documentation program will include periodic collection of feedback from volunteers and other participants on their satisfactions and ideas for improvement.

The documentation function goes on throughout the remainder of the futuring process.

Optional Tools for Preferred Futuring in a Community

In the Future Sampler Meeting (and also in the Start-Up Conference), it may help to stimulate participants' interest in thinking about the future. This can be done by exposing them to trend data from futurists and by a warm-up exercise—thinking about the distant future as a preparation for thinking about the immediate future.

- *Using futurists.* Bringing in a guest futurist or a series of them can be a good way to kick off a Preferred Futuring process in a community. The futurist should be asked to share glimpses and images of the future in general and specifically in areas relevant to the issues being considered by the community.

To stimulate participation, ask people to generate questions prior to the Future Sampler Meeting, which the futurists are asked to respond to or incorporate in their presentation. Be sure to spend some time reviewing the information and deriving implications for the future of the community.

Another technique is to assemble short articles or one-page clippings in which a futurist is commenting on an aspect of the future. Then distribute these to the group to read and discuss with regard to the relevance of each for the community as it moves into the future.

- *Warming up to thinking creatively about the future.* To help people become creative about the future—to help them take a Preferred

Future trip and think two to five years out—it may help to warm up the group by taking a longer trip first. This is similar to an activity described in Chapter Seven.

The group is briefed that they are a commission in the year 2010 preparing a report for a time capsule to be opened in the year 2500. They are asked to identify key report chapter headings, which are posted on flip chart sheets around the wall. These titles might include "Safety in the Streets," "The Impact of Technology on Family Life," "Health Care," "Economic Development," "Crime." Chapter teams are established. Everyone then wanders around and on the flip chart pages jots things that should be in each chapter that would make it a good description of the year 2010. Then teams write the major outline and ingredients of each chapter.

Phase 2: The Start-Up Conference

The Start-Up Conference will be for block or neighborhood leaders. The objectives of the conference are to provide a large number of community leaders with the following opportunities:

- To get acquainted, share ideas about the community and its future, and discover the kinds of consensus and differences that exist in the group.
- To experience the procedures of Preferred Futuring and prioritizing of images of the Preferred Future.
- To clarify their roles as supporters and leaders of the involvement of multiple groups and organizations in the community.
- To identify the groups, organizations, and populations they would like to involve in providing input and energy for future task force work.
- To recruit volunteers for tasks such as developing funding, providing leadership for futuring sessions, maintaining relations with the media, and providing training.
- To nominate a steering committee (generally seven to nine members, although steering committees can be much larger).

The agenda of the Start-Up Conference is the same as that for the Future Sampler Meeting, discussed earlier. But when asking for volunteers (the agenda's final step), a key group of volunteers are those who will be trained to convene and facilitate the Multiple Whole Community Preferred Futuring Sessions in Phase 3.

Preparing for the Start-Up Conference

The Start-Up Conference leadership must be seen as able to support an overall futuring effort, rather than as just representing some special sector of the community. A team of initiators must be responsible for designing the conference and recruiting people for the conference's leadership roles.

In preparation for the Start-Up Conference, the following activities must be done:

1. Organize a nominating session to identify key persons to be invited to the Start-Up Conference.
2. Begin locating key people who have data and knowledge about major goal areas, demographic issues, and related trends. Computerize a Resource Person Inventory with data about "Who knows what" and "What resources they can connect us to."
3. Designate the documentation team to keep the records of this Preferred Futuring and strategic planning project, and to visualize concretely the kinds of reports that will be needed in the future.
4. Plan a regular link with the media, and also plan for communication with other groups and associations.
5. Convene a Start-Up Conference team that will:
   Select the location for the Start-Up Conference and arrange for the event.
   Develop a draft design for the Start-Up Conference, review it with some potential participants, and decide on division of labor for implementation and facilitation.

Task Forces Emerging from the Start-Up Conference

As discussed earlier, several teams and committees emerge from the Start-Up Conference. The Data Collation Team will receive the data and priority images from the Preferred Futuring sessions held throughout the community (Phase 3, discussed in the next section). All this data must be reviewed, analyzed, and organized to identify emerging themes and desired future scenarios.

The Future Scenario Development Team develops scenarios from the compiled data, scenarios that will be used at the final Preferred Future Scenarios Conference.

The steering committee should identify additional resources for planning. These include previous studies done by outside agencies, businesses, departments, or governmental units that may be relevant to the futuring efforts. Individuals with specific expertise should be recruited to join the technical resource team.

Phase 3: Multiple Preferred Futuring Sessions

Preferred Futuring sessions occur in places such as school cafeterias and church basements, and they are publicized in the newspapers and other media. Each session should be convened by a team of two citizen volunteers. From past experience, let me suggest that some teams consist of an adult and a high school student; this increases participation and sends an important message.

These volunteers should receive the necessary training (one-half day to one day). An agenda for a day-long training session is presented in the example later in this chapter and in Appendix D.

Each individual Preferred Futuring session should last no more than two and a half hours. Its agenda should consist of a brief discussion about the purpose of the session and go through the following steps from the Preferred Futuring model:

- The Historical Review (a team assembles historical data before the meeting and presents it to the group
- Identifying Prouds and Sorries
- Determining Values and Beliefs
- Identifying Events, Developments, and Trends
- Developing the Preferred Future Vision

The data from these sessions, as discussed earlier, are used to develop future scenarios, which are used at the Scenarios Conference—Phase 4.

Phase 4: The Preferred Futures Scenarios Conference

The Preferred Futures Scenarios Conference is basically a day-long town meeting, which can be attended by anyone in the community. At this meeting, the data from the Multiple Preferred Futuring sessions is presented, the Preferred Vision is ratified, and strategic priorities are set with next steps and responsibilities identified.

The Scenarios Conference has the following agenda:

1. Presentation by the Future Scenarios Development Team of the priority future visions.
2. Discussion about whether these visions are really priorities, after which the entire group agrees what their visions will be.
3. Creating Action Goals and an Action Plan to implement these visions.
4. Setting up ongoing volunteer committees to carry out the action steps.

Planning the Scenarios Conference

The planning for the Scenarios Conference includes three major types of activities:

• *Design of the conference and making arrangements.* Tasks include selecting leadership for the day, planning the activities, developing handout materials and packets, and arranging for documentation of the events and evaluation. In addition, volunteers must be coached or briefed to help facilitate the conference.

• *Logistical and coordination arrangements.* Tasks include sending invitations, arranging for promotion and media coverage, registration, on-site equipment, supplies, food service, and child care.

- *Development of follow-up and continuity support structures.* Tasks include developing financial, clerical, and technical support that task forces emerging from the conference will need; structures for training in techniques of effective meetings and teamwork; and establishing a documentation team and tools.

Now let us see how this process was used by a community.

An Example of a Community Using Preferred Futuring

The story begins with a director of county planning in a Midwest state. This particular county was a beautiful tourist area, and much of its prosperity and growth was based on this fact. The planning director had become very aware of the way unplanned and unchecked development was destroying this most precious resource. And he was frustrated by his inability to influence the townships within the county to realize their common problem and to act as a whole system. Instead townships would compete and fight with each other, concerned with their own individual growth, well-being, and share of the economic pie. And the erosion of natural beauty just continued.

Using newspaper advertisements, the planning director put together a subcommittee of concerned citizens and finally asked our company for help. We worked with him and his staff and volunteers as they created a whole-systems planning process.

The futuring process followed several phases.

Phase 1: The Future Sampler Meeting

A group of leaders and respected figures were invited to a Future Sampler Meeting where the planning director's concerns were presented and participants experienced a sample of the proposed solution. The two-and-a-half-hour meeting agenda generally followed the one discussed earlier in the chapter for Future Sampler Meetings, and included:

- Welcome
- View from the planning department
- History of situation
- Current Prouds and Sorries
- Demonstration of the proposed futuring process
- A sampler of the Preferred Futuring process that helped them create a Preferred Future vision
- Proposal for countywide involvement at each township level
- Questions, answers, and discussion

The participants in the Future Sampler Meeting concluded with agreement to move forward with the Preferred Futuring process by nominating respected grassroots leaders in each township and planning the next steps.

After the Future Sampler Meeting, the steering committee was formed, and it finalized the goals for the project:

- Gather input and ideas from citizens throughout the county.
- Compile this feedback, informing township, city, county officials, and citizens of the results.
- Employ citizen input in the revision of the County Master Plan, development of growth guidelines, and transportation plan.
- Help promote cooperation and communication among all units of government.

The planning group's motto: *"The best way to predict the future is to invent it."*

Phase 2: A Start-Up Conference

Volunteers from the Future Sampler Meeting helped plan and invite representative township stakeholders to the next meeting—a Start-Up Conference. In all cases formal invitations were followed up with personal contact. Sometimes this included multiple contacts and personal arm twisting.

The conference was larger than the Future Sampler Meeting, but the agenda was similar. And it included a decision to go forward. At the conference, there were nominations of respected leaders in each township who would be helpful supporters in the process and others who would be good volunteers to work on implementation.

Phase 3: Multiple Preferred Futuring Events

Volunteers convened and facilitated Preferred Futuring sessions countywide. Prior to the futuring sessions, these volunteers were invited to a one-day training session. The agenda (which is a standard approach for orienting and training volunteers) included:

- Welcome
- The history of the situation and the current concern
- The steps leading up to today
- The plan and why you are here, including questions (from small table groups comprising participants who represent a diverse group) and answers
- A sample of Preferred Futuring, including the power of whole-systems thinking
- Lunch break
- Preferred Futuring convener training
  Responsibility of a convener
  Skills of a convener
  The format for a Preferred Futuring community meeting
  Necessary materials and logistics
  How to deal with skepticism and distrust and how to build on
    optimism and positive attitudes
  Nuts and bolts of the countywide process and the time line
  The next steps in the process and the support available

A more complete agenda for the afternoon is provided in Appendix D.

Documentation and Support

The county planning office coordinated the project efforts, provided logistical support, and was the repository of township Preferred Future scenarios information. By this time a steering committee of twenty-four people had been formed. The town meeting Preferred Futuring facilitators numbered thirty. There was an additional cadre of fifteen "general members" who were involved in helping to choreograph and execute the project.

The planning office and cadre of volunteers then produced a whole-county vision and sponsored a county plenary session (a Scenarios Conference) to review and ratify the results, and plan follow-up action.

The Scenarios Conference occurred along the lines of the agenda presented earlier in this chapter, in the section on Phase 4, the Preferred Futuring Scenarios Conference.

The Results of This Futuring Process

After the Scenarios Conference, the planning department shifted its view of its role from planning *for* the county to planning *with* the county. The 163-page report summarized the information from all the futuring sessions and the Scenarios Conference. The report's cover letter is worth sharing:

> Dear citizens,
>
> One of the major purposes of government is to maintain and enhance the quality of life for all citizens. We strive to achieve this through a variety of methods including: law enforcement, public services, utilities, and land use planning. One of the major tools used in planning and zoning is the county's comprehensive land use plan.
>
> Last year when the County Planning Commission began the process of updating the Master Plan they reached a very important decision. The new County Comprehensive Plan should contain more than facts, maps, and statistical projections. It should be a living document, which reflects attitudes, opinions, and values of the citizens of this county.
>
> This report summarizes the opinions and attitudes gathered throughout the county during 20 futuring sessions held September through December. It will be used as the basis for the Comprehensive Land Use Plan and other activities aimed at better growth management.

On behalf of the County Board of Commissioners, I thank you for your interest and participation in this program. We believe that greater citizen involvement in government will lead to better planning. We look forward to your continuing interest and involvement in the future of our county.

Sincerely,
Chairman, County Board of Commissioners

This letter reflected the shift in how the planning department perceived its responsibilities (from writers of the plan to facilitators of the plan).

The department's report was organized as follows:

- Goals of the project
- A description of the Preferred Futuring process
- History of the area
- What we are most proud of and sorry about
- Future images and the percentage of interest in each image
- Individual township results
- Demographics
- Press clippings containing pictures and descriptions of the process

The Preferred Future visions were about future states in these areas: agriculture, environment, pollution, art, government, recycling, beauty, housing, safety, development and growth, people and quality of life, transportation, downtown historical preservation, health, trees and forests, economic development and tourism, planning, parks and recreation, education, zoning, and water quality.

In addition to mobilizing citizen involvement and building a greater whole-systems perspective, some concrete steps emerged:

- The report was distributed and stimulated widespread interest, creating ripples of action throughout the whole system. Neighboring townships began to work jointly, and committees of concerned citizens from different counties began to function. The whole county became aware of the world as seen through the eyes of each township.

- With the assistance of the Preferred Futuring process, the steering committee and township planning officials drafted a growth guideline book. This forged a new partnership between the township planners and the county planners.

- A formal, countywide survey of residents was conducted that focused on the key issues identified in the project and based on growth management alternatives outlined in the growth guidelines book.

- A program of community education about the content, use, and implementation of the growth guideline book was initiated by a volunteer committee that emerged from the Preferred Futuring process.

Overall Time Line

It may be helpful to put the activities in this example into a time line:

Month	Activity
0–3	Goals, objectives and purpose of the project are published in the newspaper, and the citizen volunteers who respond and the planning department form the initial sub-committee.
4–5	Volunteers research the citizen feedback programs in other communities.
5–6	The county selects the Preferred Futuring method because of its positive, proactive focus on the future; the consultant is retained; and the Future Sampler Meeting is held.
6–7	Start-Up Conference is held at Civic Center; a facilitator training session is held; and the first few Preferred Futuring sessions are held.
7–8	Additional Preferred Futuring sessions held in Ecumenical Assembly Hall and Audubon Society, including a session for the League of Women Voters.
8–9	Remaining township futuring sessions are held, as well as futuring sessions for T.C. High School students and Hotel and Motel Association members.
9–10	Reports on futuring sessions are returned to Township Boards, and the County Board of Commissioners receives final whole-system report.

10–13   The final report is presented at the Scenarios Conference and distributed to all townships. Follow-up activities continue.

It took over a year to complete the whole process on a county-wide level. But it took nine months once the consultant began the process with the system. We have seen it take about this same amount of time with cities.

TIPS FOR PREFERRED FUTURING IN A COMMUNITY

When Preferred Futuring is done in a community, here are some basic conditions for success and some traps to be avoided:

1. The start-up group should use a sound nomination process to identify and recruit a network of key influential individuals from all sectors of the community.

A trap is to focus on only the financial and political "influentials" or leave out very new or retired people.

2. Conduct Preferred Futuring sessions with an all-inclusive sample of stakeholder groups within the community. Thus feedback includes concrete future images of improved quality of life, economic developments, improvements in political organization, civil enterprise, and so on. In addition to open sessions, all groups in an area should have an opportunity to request such a session to provide their input.

A typical trap is holding a conference of a limited number of leaders who become the brain trust for the community, and who then assume, "We can get the others to come aboard later after we decide what is needed." This must not happen.

3. Staff task forces must identify the key resource experts in various areas of future planning within the community, and use them effectively.

A typical trap is to assume that experts will identify themselves and offer their know-how appropriately. This is not the usual pattern for many resource specialists.

4. In preparation for the Scenarios Conference, the rich pluralism of Preferred Future images from the Multiple Preferred Futuring sessions must be converted into concrete scenarios of "what it would look like if . . . " and dramatically presented to those who have participated in the input and to others who might get interested at this stage.

A typical trap is to condense and abstract the future images so they lose concreteness or richness of imagery. In this abstract form, they do not attract and inspire volunteers to form action task forces to help create the preferred future.

5. Recruit the financial supports and personal commitments to follow through on making things happen after priority goals have been identified.

A typical trap is to stimulate enthusiastic participants and then fail to guide and train volunteers. This training helps the volunteers learn to cope with resistance, to generate momentum for follow-up action, and to conduct exciting meetings.

Conclusion

I believe Preferred Futuring is the most powerful tool we have for operating democratically. It brings together the broadest possible community representation to shape the future, empowering people to choose a Preferred Future rather than merely let the future happen. I am reminded of a small town in Nova Scotia that we had helped successfully complete a planning and citizen involvement process that was seen as very successful. A year later the Provincial government was holding a hearing to get citizen support for placing a nuclear power plant in a region close to this town. It would in fact raise the water temperature in the large lake where local commercial aquaculture was in progress. The government allegedly had people planted in the audience to assure a desired positive conclusion. But it was the citizens of this small town who initiated and garnered local citizen support to block the plans to locate the power plant in that region. They were instrumental in empowering other local communities to successfully assert their will. I am still deeply moved as I think about this story. This is the kind of empowerment, large scale, that can result from Preferred Futuring. It heals and strengthens the human spirit at various micro and macro levels and in various ways.

14

Knowing When to Use Preferred Futuring

There are some things to which you don't want to adapt. We can invent. We can consciously create our own and collective future of choice. What is it? Who will shape it?

First, Diagnose the Need

It is easy to become very excited about the potentialities of human energy and creativity that the Preferred Futuring process will unleash and focus. But while Preferred Futuring is a powerful paradigm and tool, it certainly may not be called for in every situation; it is important to consider its intelligent use. To diagnose the need for Preferred Futuring when vision or action steps are needed, there are two models that I have found useful: the Change Model and the Transition Model.

The Change Model

The Change Model consists of the following formula:

$$C = D \times V \times F > R$$

Change (C) occurs when Dissatisfaction (D), Vision (V), and First Steps of Action (F) exceed Resistance (R).[1] This formula helps explain why change happens or does not happen when a change effort is mounted, and what is necessary for success.

Components of the Model

Change (C) means to move from one state to another, to become different from what was. In this formula, change is dependent on only four things—Dissatisfaction, Vision, First Steps, and Resistance.

People must be dissatisfied with the way things are now. Dissatisfaction then can be used as a lever for change. Unfortunately, dissatisfaction often takes the form of complaints about the way things are now, expressed with the belief that nothing can be done. Some people seem quite convinced of, and even cling to, their helplessness and victimhood. I call this living in the world of "ain't it awful." With all due respect, this situation may be the obvious result of living in a system where for years people have been treated as if they were not capable of intelligent decisions. But we all must eventually let go of this and become responsible for the future we want.

Letting go may also involve helping leadership decide to let go of control as their part in this organizational shift.

Dissatisfaction thus needs to be transformed into motivation for change. The focus must shift from the problem to the desired future—to the V or Vision part of the formula. This is done by asking, "Well, what *do* you want?" This leads us to the second determinant of change: Vision. Vision is a clear, specific, detailed, and agreed-upon picture of the future that people are willing to align with and to focus all their energy on to accomplish.

It is important to realize that V does not mean the vision that leaders carry around and occasionally share with select people, or the vision that they try to push down through the organization. Neither is it the variety of different, individual visions that a leadership team carries around and operates from, visions that the team members don't openly share with each other, which result in their operating at cross-purposes to each other. V refers to a collective and detailed picture of a future that everyone in an organization or community wants.

The third determinant of change is First Steps, the action plans and concrete steps that help the system move from vision to implementation actions. At various levels this can look like a strategic plan based on a collective vision and including specific strategic initiatives with assigned responsibilities, or it can look like departmental annual goals and action plans based on a departmental vision that is aligned with the total organization vision, or it can look like the specific steps to implement a new work process that is aligned with strategic departmental and organization quality vision priorities.

When you have Dissatisfaction, Vision, and First Steps, Resistance is greatly reduced and the product of D, V, and F will be greater than R; change will occur. For example, if you help people let go of "ain't it awful" and move to the excitement of deciding what they do want, R is reduced by a large factor. If people participate in a process that determines the direction of the organization and events in their immediate workplace, that reduces R by an even larger factor. And if people's energy is focused on planning and removing the blocks to taking action, specific resistances can be confronted in the system and in people in a very focused way; this reduces R by another factor. By then R has been transformed into productive energy.

Notice that these components D, V, and F are multiplicative. If any one is missing, the value then becomes zero in that part of the equation, and the product of D, V, and F will not be greater than R. And change becomes unlikely.

Using the Model

To elaborate on the point just made, if V equals zero—if there is no vision—change is unlikely to occur. Thus the Change Model helps determine when to use Preferred Futuring, because it shows those situations where V (vision) or F (action steps) is missing or insufficiently clear.

Here are several examples.

First, dissatisfaction may be high in a system, but there is no Preferred Future vision and no First Steps (action plan). There may be lots of griping about "what is," but there is no clear notion of what people do want as an alternative. Sometimes there is no unified or agreed-upon current state—but lots of secret opinions. There are lots of turf-oriented behaviors and suboptimization between units.

A Preferred Futuring process can provide the necessary alignment and create conditions for teamwork and wider systems thinking. It can give V a value, and thus help overcome resistance (R).

Second, there may be enough dissatisfaction to stimulate action and there may be some First Steps, but with no clear Preferred Future vision. This is often referred to as the *knee-jerk* reaction. People often say, "We have identified problem X . . . right? . . . okay, let's do Y." This generally leads to ill-informed action with no lasting change and increased feelings of failure. This is too often done on a grand scale regarding systemwide issues, leading to "flavor of the month" dynamics in a system and creating swings back and forth with no apparent strategy or direction.

Third, a department or organization may have dissatisfaction and an abundance of creative and visionary clarity, with no concrete first steps or support structures. This leads to an inability to take action on a clear direction, and high frustration. Things never quite get off the ground.

In a variation on this, an organization's dissatisfaction may have led to developing a vision (V), but there is lots of frustration due to lack of implementation or action steps. People may not understand or agree with a vision of the leader. Or the visioning process they used lacked specificity as well as widespread involvement. In this case it is necessary to revisit the vision, make it more concrete and specific, assure widespread involvement and then involve people in the action planning steps.

This last situation is often the most difficult condition. People will express their resistance as, "we already visioned before, but it didn't work—nothing changed." Until people have experienced real Preferred Futuring, it is difficult for them to understand the difference.

The Change Model helps identify where essential elements are missing or not sufficiently developed, and thus change is not taking place.

The Transition Model

The Transition Model can also indicate the appropriateness of Preferred Futuring.[2] It is clear to me that anytime there has been a change in the life of a system, a transition situation is created—a temporary period while the system moves from where it was before some event or onset of new conditions to a new state. This is often likened to the metaphor of crossing a river, as shown in Figure 14.1. Successful transitions contain some basic steps of letting go and stepping off the familiar ground and moving through chaotic, unchartered territory and arriving at a desired new territory, just like crossing a river.

Thus, before the new change can be embraced, the first necessary step is letting go—letting go of old baggage and comfort with the way things have been, comfort that will hold us back. Letting go of the old processes or people we used to work with or old beliefs such as "Only leadership is responsible" or "We are all in competition with other departments for the scarce resources," and so on. In many cases a process of mourning may be appropriate.

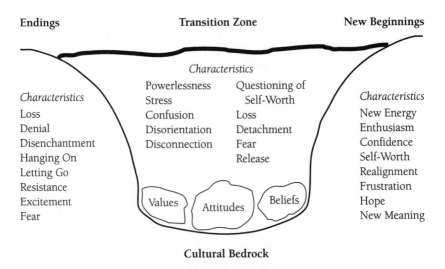

Figure 14.1 The Transition Model

This transition time can be very scary and confusing to people throughout the system. People can feel lost and have a sense of failure. The confusion and fear can be blamed on co-workers or on oneself. Or on leadership, which is accused of not knowing where it is going.

What is not understood is that confusion is a natural part of the transition. I usually view confusion as a positive diagnostic sign that the transition is under way. We have also noticed that those who have been dealing with the transition the longest, often leadership, have the vision of the other side of the river and even make the emotional crossing and arrive at the far bank while many people are still on the old bank or are in the river making the crossing, fully experiencing the uncertainty. Those who arrive at the new bank may exhort the others to let go, to get in the water and come along, and then become frustrated with the resistance they encounter.

Using the Transition Model

Sometimes if a system in transition has a high level of resistance, with lots of frustration and confusion at all levels, it often helps to create or reaffirm the vision in more detail. This clarifies what the other riverbank looks like—where the organization is headed. Affirming a Preferred Future Vision often dramatically transforms the fear of the unknown and the resistance into excitement and motivated efforts to achieve the new state; it can help move the whole organization across the river to the new bank in a much more profound, orderly, unified, simultaneous, and uplifting manner. This also provides a context for a temporary transition plan to get to the new organization. And it helps everyone in a system agree about where they all want to arrive on the new bank, and helps them explore and decide what they need to bring and leave behind.

Occasionally the whole system may be in a state of shock and confusion, having been thrown into transition abruptly by extreme internal or external events. Catharsis and healing are needed. Slightly modifying the Preferred Futuring steps to allow more than usual catharsis while reviewing the past (the Historical Review) and listing Prouds and Sorries can provide the needed healing and grounding so that people can position themselves to talk about the future they want. This helps people pull the pieces together, organize themselves, and strike off across the river together toward a new and desirable alternative.

Conclusion

When change is being attempted, the Change Model may indicate that there is no vision of the future or that it lacks specificity. Or it may indicate that the steps to implement it are missing. These are indications that Preferred Futuring can be useful.

When a system is moving from one situation to another and experiences strong resistance, this also indicates that Preferred Futuring is appropriate as a way of dealing with the resistance.

15

Applying Preferred Futuring in a Variety of Situations

Creation is not over. It is barely under way. In ten thousand years we may be colonizing planets all over the galaxy. Twenty-fifth-century people will look back at twentieth-century primitives. There is more to come. The exciting and beautiful thing about it is we have been given an opportunity to consciously participate.

Creating a Broad-Based Strategic Plan

This book has included numerous examples of Preferred Futuring. In this chapter I want to show how it can be specifically applied to effect positive outcomes in areas such as strategic planning, process improvement, conflict management, and even personal and spiritual development.

In most traditional strategic planning processes, a small group in charge of strategic planning writes the plan or a consultant is hired to write the plan. Then the plan is communicated to the rest of the system for implementation. This has been a notoriously poor approach; the plan typically sits on a shelf (gathering dust and guilt, and without affecting decisions) until the next strategic plan is written.

Preferred Futuring introduces two important aspects missing in traditional strategic planning. First, it focuses on a specific desired future state, a focus that results in some benefits key to effective planning:

- We move from predictions to plans and hopes.
- We create a condition for tapping creativity, innovation, and breakthroughs.
- We capture people's imagination, passions, and excitement, creating energy for taking action and motivation for commitment and follow-through.

Second, we involve extremely large numbers in the planning process, resulting in some other key outcomes:

- By involving all stakeholders in the planning process, we use all the brainpower and resources of the system and create a higher-quality plan and goals for action.
- During the planning process—in real time—there is a widespread understanding of the whole system, of each subpart's impact on the whole, and of the plan. This increases teamwork, cooperation, and efficiency.
- There is an immediate, intelligent, coordinated, and timely systemwide implementation of the plan, saving time and money.
- This broad-based involvement, understanding, and implementation stimulates a high level of motivation and commitment to making the plan work throughout the system.

It seems obvious that any effective planning process must include successful implementation as a component. Unfortunately, in most strategic planning processes, just producing the plan seems to be enough. The Preferred Futuring process produces a high-quality plan for which the implementation has been included and is already under way. This is strategic planning in real time. The strategic plan now becomes a living document and can drive the business plans. It may also grow and shift in an organic way as the whole system grows and shifts with internal growth and learning and with changing environmental conditions, such as new customer demands and new available resources.

The Real-Time Strategic Planning Model

Figure 15.1 shows a model for using Preferred Futuring in strategic planning.[1] Steps 1 through 5 occur at the Preferred Futuring event, with the other steps occurring subsequently. The strategic planning event, indicated by the dark-lined box, can take from two to three days, depending on the number of people involved, the logistics, and the process required to achieve the specific deliverables desired. (Overlaying this model, of course, are the preplanning, leadership preparation, microcosm design team effort, and follow-up support discussed earlier.)

Let me briefly explain each step.

1. *Scan externally and internally.* A scan of the environment and stakeholders provides a common understanding of the environment and the stakeholders' needs. The environment is made up of market trends, new technology, competitors, economic trends, and workforce trends. Stakeholders are the external customers, board members, corporate suppliers, division and unit leadership, middle managers, union leadership, and workers. An internal scan of the current state includes Prouds and Sorries, decision-making processes, and so on.

These scans can be done creatively with the top several layers of a large organization present. They can include panel interviews of customers and other stakeholders, information from future trend experts, and table group information sharing what is known about current internal processes across the entire gathering. Feedback can be given about how people are making each other's jobs harder and what would be needed to change this. The information generated becomes part of the record for use in planning. Establishing this common database is a required first step.

2. *Affirm mission and strategic direction.* It is crucial at the beginning of the planning process to answer the question, What business are we in? The mission should be reviewed and discussed to assure a common understanding. At this point, the leadership team can review the old strategic plan and strategic objectives or even offer a draft plan.

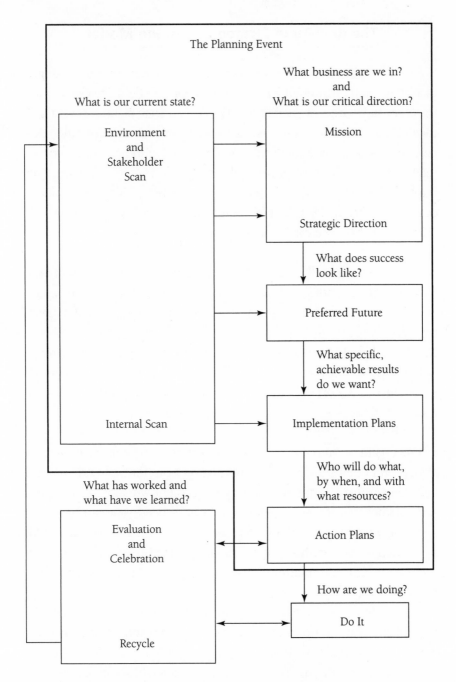

Figure 15.1 The Real-Time Strategic Planning Model

If this is done, there needs to be time for discussion and the asking of clarifying questions, and then table groups can talk about changes.

3. *Develop the Preferred Future.* The whole group is asked to develop a picture of what the organization would be doing and what stakeholders would be saying that indicates success and pleases them, if they have realized the mission and carried out the plan. This information gets shared and strategic priorities with a five- to ten-year time frame are affirmed, modified, and more deeply understood. This clarifies strategic focus or direction and sets strategic goals.

4. *Develop action plans.* Cross-functional groups working simultaneously develop the who, what, how, and when steps to achieve the desired strategic results. These need to be action plans that can be started upon return to the workplace. And these action plans must include a monitoring and support function for the implementation activities.

5. *Develop implementation plans and strategies.* Functional groups now assess the tasks awaiting them back on the job and determine what individuals and teams must start to do differently next week to make this strategic planning meeting successful. These become strategic objectives with a one- to two-year time frame. They are worded to be achievable and to produce measurable results.

6. *Create an implementation structure.* This phase, which occurs during or after the Preferred Futuring event, is most successful if there is a continued coordination and support function in each unit as well as at the top of the organization. The best way to do this is a cascade-down, in which the process is replicated with the remaining layers of the organization on a unit-by-unit basis. The remaining layers add their more specific and operational pieces to the whole picture. First-line stakeholders are much more interested in and possess key resources for determining specific implementation and action plans relevant to daily customer needs. A cascade-down works best when units use the strategic plans and objectives as a basis for their yearly business plans.

7. *Evaluate and recycle.* Accountability and support procedures need to be built into all action plans. Evaluation data must be used for

improvement purposes only. One of the key and most overlooked implementation and evaluation activities is celebrating. Small wins, minor successes, and concrete milestones need to be acknowledged or claimed and celebrated. This helps make evaluation part of implementation and provides additional motivational energy during the tough times of implementation.

The evaluative data can be recycled yearly at the business planning process level. This can include a yearly review and modification of the strategic plan and business plan. This helps keep the strategic plan a living document and links it to the business plan.

This Preferred Futuring–based Strategic Planning Model assumes that, to make a difference, planning must include implementation and must be an interactive process involving all key stakeholders, including implementers. The model allows strategic planning to occur with large numbers of stakeholders and in real time. It creates a broad base of support for the strategic plan, and substantially increases its chance of being implemented successfully.

Preferred Futuring as a Management Tool

Preferred Futuring is a useful tool when a leader is wearing the hat of coach or supervisor. Here is a summary of some applications to help you think of ways to apply it in your situation:

- *Setting performance goals.* When you are working with an employee to set performance goals, a Preferred Future brainstorming session with the two of you can produce specific, mutually exciting pictures of success and success criteria. For example, Prouds and Sorries concerning past performance and a Preferred Future vision of success can be more motivating than looking at shortfalls and setting new goals to "fix" the situation.
- *Setting department goals.* When you are developing departmental yearly goals, Preferred Futuring allows you to involve all members

of the department. You can tap into their specific knowledge and creativity and produce goals that members will understand, be committed to, and accomplish even if a stretch is required.

- *Improving work flow.* When you are dealing with an unsatisfactory work situation, Preferred Futuring provides a way to describe what a work situation would look like if the identified dissatisfaction was remedied. This helps establish a collective picture of an exciting resolution with clear success criteria. The energy put into complaining or focusing on what is wrong or acting in a powerless manner is redirected into productive action alternatives.

- *Green field planning.* When you are preparing to build a new facility, Preferred Futuring provides strategic operational information for facility layout and breakthrough decisions on setup and operations. Preferred Futuring provides a way to elicit key information from stakeholders so architects can design a facility that will support effective work processes.

Preferred Futuring is a powerful and robust tool for a manager or supervisor who believes everyone has a key role to play in creative solutions and implementation. It is very useful for beginning to move a team or whole department from helpless victim consciousness toward becoming self-empowered partners.

Preferred Futuring as a Process Improvement Tool

Preferred Futuring can help focus a process improvement effort, providing a way to gain stakeholder involvement and stimulate innovation during process redesign.

The special education and social services staff of an intermediate school district had asked for a retreat to improve the quality of the services to their customers.

We started by asking them, "Who is your customer?" It turned out that opinions differed as to whether customers were children, parents, taxpayers, teachers, or the board of education. This was a complex issue. By "putting on the hat" of each of these constituency groups and doing a Preferred Future as if each of those groups was in the room, the staff began to clarify needs that were common themes and special to one or more constituent groups. They were able to identify some needed improvements to delivering services. They also discovered, by this Preferred Futuring exercise, that they needed to go out and gather more data from certain customer groups. The exercise created a breakthrough on bringing the group together around a set of strategic priorities for process improvement and clear next steps.

Using Conflict and Diversity Productively

Conflict is one of the most avoided aspects of organizational and group life. People often seem to believe that conflict will lead to damaged relationships, destroyed trust, or open warfare if addressed. But in reality, conflict is most costly when avoided, creating loss of communication and contact, low energy or morale, low creativity, resentment toward others, backstabbing, and tension. All this blocks energy from flowing into the organization's objectives and field of creative energy.

It is important to understand that conflict is a fact of life and an important source of energy, creativity, and innovation—and that it is likely to increase in times of change.

Preferred Futuring has often helped oppositional parties or factions to find common cause and move ahead together. Here are two examples of how it can work.

A Town Moves from Conflict to a Collective High

A small town in Canada was a central point in a tourist route. It had a waterfront area to be preserved, merchant businesses to be developed, a tourist trade to be developed, and beautiful natural resources and fine quality of life to be maintained. Which of these was "the most important issue" and what was the "answer" depended on who you spoke to.

The town had initiated a planning process with a series of committees to work on these various issues, but conflict between many of the committees emerged within the first eight months. These committees and the citizenry now planned to come together in a plenary session to develop the community's long-range plan. Leadership had achieved a high level of citizen involvement. Yet there was also real fear and trepidation that the plenary session would erupt into violent shouting matches as each committee put forth its rival proposal.

Prior to the plenary session, the town asked me and my colleague for help. We in turn asked each committee to translate its proposal into a detailed vision of how things would look five years from now if the proposal was implemented. The day before the plenary session, there was tension up and down Main Street. The town clerk, a significant figure in the process and the politics, was openly very negative about the chances of success. This did not bode well.

We met in the hall above the fire station. The event began with a review of the town's history and milestones in its growth and development. Some old-timers were interviewed as part of this process. Then we reviewed the reason for initiating the planning process a year ago and forming the committees. Reports of each committee's vision (but not their proposals) were given. Suggestions from the floor to the committee visions were recorded but not discussed.

The committees were asked to consider these suggestions and modify their vision as they wished. During this time caucuses and side communications across committees were encouraged where it seemed relevant. A more whole-system view began to emerge. Later committee reports included the new vision and the implementation plans.

This event did not go without heated discussion and venting at times. But it did result in the entire town aligning around a common vision and a series of proposed actions that formed the entire strategic and action plan. It seemed to me that under the surface some old wounds were healed and new alliances formed.

Walking down Main Street the next morning was an entirely different experience. The whole town was high. This still remains a most exciting and proud memory.

A School Faculty Agrees to Disagree, and Kids Win
This is the only time in my experience when the conflict apparently could not be resolved through a common vision for the system. It

began when a small elementary school in a midstate New York school system where I was working at the time asked me for help. The school administration wanted to resolve a deep and bitter conflict that divided the faculty and consumed considerable energy, energy that could have gone into the effective education of children.

This process began with some initial data gathering. It became clear that the faculty was deeply divided on the issue of the method of teaching: a more structured, teacher-centered method versus a less structured, student-centered method. An initial futuring process resulted in two very distinctly different future images with equal amounts of support. And educational research indicated that the reasons cited by both factions had validity.

But as a result of the Preferred Futuring process, the two visions became clearly articulated. This made it possible to establish success criteria for both visions. And the two factions agreed to treat each one as an experimental hypothesis. They agreed to set up their programs as they wished in the two separate wings of the school building. They committed to assess their progress toward each of the visions and share this on a regular interim and yearly basis.

The result: Both programs were successful and provided opportunities for children who needed more structure or needed more openness due to their individual learning styles. This was a true win-win situation.

In the process of involving a broad group of stakeholders and creating a common database, Preferred Futuring creates common ground, a common ground that can help heal conflict and allow the organization or community to move into the future together.

Fostering Personal and Spiritual Growth

So far, this book has dealt with Preferred Futuring as a process applied to groups. But it can also be applied to individuals to foster their personal and spiritual growth. And since any organization or group obviously consists of individuals, I feel strongly that some mention of the personal side of Preferred Futuring is appropriate.

Personal Growth

In the area of personal growth and realizing one's potential, there is a common theme: develop a positive self-image in a particular area of personal ability or of life. Preferred Futuring is a powerful tool for this. The Preferred Futuring process is ideal for personal life planning. The focus can be anything from a future career or job situation to having more joy and love in one's life. But it is usually helpful to limit the scope to a certain area of life, such as your relationship with your spouse or work partner or sibling or parent, or with your job or financial situation.

The Preferred Futuring process that an individual goes through closely follows that already described. In the historical review, you review the evolutionary steps and milestones to arriving at the current state of your needs and abilities. Then you create a time line tracing emotional, cognitive, and spiritual highs and lows during your life. This often illustrates that a memorable time or event that may have been emotionally traumatic (a low) may have led to or been associated with a time of cognitive emotional or spiritual growth. This helps provide a perspective that what felt like a misfortune may have had an upside to it.

In analyzing your current state, simply identify what you are proud or sorry about in your current situation. This could include anything from a significant relationship or work situation to the amount of joy or pain in your life and so on. I have found that soliciting data and asking for feedback from others is a valuable part of this process. If there are others who will be affected by accomplishing your preferred future, it is often a good idea to include them at relevant points during planning and implementation.

The events, trends, and developments assessment can be an eye-opener. It is always illuminating to ask what future developments might occur in this relationship or situation. New realizations may occur that are liberating or strategic, such as this person will continue to abuse you or that person seems to be growing more distant or is attempting to become closer and more caring. It might become clearer that the work situation actually offers some very positive aspects of life—or is draining all your energy.

Defining your future vision is a step that needs to be done with no holds barred. You must reach deep into your soul and allow preferred images of potential to bubble up and be acknowledged. Images must be prioritized from an open, "anything is possible" psychological state. Once they are identified they can be reality-tested and modified. Loved ones and best friends can often see much more wonderful possibilities than we can. So it is often rewarding and helpful to include their images of potential for us before we create the specific Action Goals.

In creating your Action Plan, rather than starting with a large, all-encompassing and difficult step, I suggest starting with only a single simple and doable step.

Also critical is developing commitment to action and soliciting the support of friends or other significant persons in your life. Your will may weaken from time to time, and an external support system can make a big difference.

Spiritual Growth

The major difference between personal growth and a focus on purely spiritual growth is nothing but a consciousness shift. You realize that you are not just a physical being but a spiritual being—a soul. You must now face squarely the premise that you have the power to choose and that transformation is a possibility. If you remember quantum physics, it is the attention and expectation that transforms existing matter into energy and into new matter again. If you believe it can be so, your intent will align you with the reality you want to create.

The steps are simple and vary only slightly from those of personal growth. They involve moving into a whole-systems view, realizing that we are part of and interconnected with a larger system—that we have an impact on it as it does on us.

The steps are as follows:

1. *Consciously and unequivocally choose to create the desired future state.* It is not important to know the details at this point. For example, "I choose to be in a joyful rather than a painful relationship" is quite enough. "I choose to be healed of my whiplash" could be fine also.

2. *Articulate "What I want to change is. . . ."* Then describe a current condition that has become a priority and your feelings and perceptions about it. For example, "This relationship is very hurtful to me. I have been trying to make it right. I am only hurting and resenting more deeply. It prevents me from having a fulfilling, intimate relationship and from having joy in my life."

3. *Identify "What is prompting my decision to change at this time is. . . ."* It is very important to identify the motivation for change. Does it come from an internal source? Does it come from wanting to stop being a victim or moving toward breaking a co-dependency? Or is it externally motivated? "Everyone is talking about joy, so I had better do this to be 'with it' in my conversations with my friends."

4. *Identify "How I am contributing to the situation is. . . ."* If you are in a relationship, possibly you are trying to have the other person live up to your standards rather than theirs, or maybe you have been trying to fix up this relationship and are not willing to let go. Possibly you don't believe you deserve to be in a joyful relationship. This should be a gentle process and not include any blaming.

5. *As in the Prouds and Sorries exercise, you can identify what being in this situation keeps you from doing or having or becoming, and what it currently allows you to be or do or have.* For example, "It stops me from having more energy and love to invest in my life and it provides me with the familiar role of fixer in the situation, just like I had in my family when I was young." This helps you begin to identify and release the old pattern with its particular energy or frequency.

6. *Now determine the Preferred Future.* Identify "What inner experience and outer manifestation do I really want to create? What if this relationship was instantly transformed—what do I want? What would I have? Who would I be? What would I be impelled to do?" This helps you create the new pattern with a different energetic frequency that will draw you toward a future you prefer.

7. *Allow actions to emerge, and observe any new behaviors or attitudes that may seem to spontaneously manifest.* You can choose to be on the edge of life—to be a spectator—or you can consciously plan and execute actions. A change will take place in how you experience the

world. As you act on your new positive choice you may find yourself more aligned with a sense of inner purpose.

Remember, daring to dream or ask for the best *is* the most powerful way to identify and break through resistance to spiritual growth. A Preferred Future statement helps you be as specific and graphic as possible. This surfaces the resistances so that you can let them go and become more whole or healed.

Here are some tips for this process:

• Take the seed thought of the future you want into meditation or prayer and allow answers, strategies, solutions, useful understandings, or insights to come to you.

• Write the whole vision statement down, review it frequently, add to or modify it as you go.

• Summarize your vision statement into a one-liner or phrase so you can easily declare your intention to have or create it.

• Declare your intention wholeheartedly and without reservations or disclaimers.

• Allow the vision time to manifest, and notice and celebrate the milestones along the way.

• Be open to and document learnings and deeper understandings that will come from the process you have invoked.

Just as we have seen how Preferred Futuring can be a very direct way to the core of any organization or large whole system, it can also be a very direct way to our personal center as a whole system. It is an important resource for the care and nurturing of our soul.

Conclusion

I am periodically impressed with the incredible robustness of the Preferred Futuring process. By robust I mean that it almost seems impervious to failure under about any conditions. It just seems to work! At its core is the paradigm shift from identifying problems to identifying the future we want. It is that basic and fundamental shift that we have to take in and assimilate. Once we grasp that point, it becomes quite easy to adapt the Preferred Futuring steps and methods to many different situations. Then comes the exciting and creative act of making up new methods for new challenges to help whole systems use the steps to create the future they are passionate about and build the pathways to that future together.

I do believe that each time we use Preferred Futuring in this way something special takes place. Human energy is unleashed as a whole human system becomes aligned body and soul, heart and mind, to generate the energy field that creates something awesome. This I feel is empowering. It often moves me deeply. It often feels like a gift to have participated.

PART 4

Looking Ahead

Parts Two and Three of this book illustrated how Preferred Futuring creates within an organization or system of any size an environment that facilitates activities as diverse as strategic planning and setting performance standards for an individual. In Part Four, Chapter Sixteen looks at the implications of using Preferred Futuring for leadership in meeting today's challenges. Then Chapter Seventeen discusses why Preferred Futuring works—how it creates a field of generative energy that links it with the new science and spirit in the workplace.

16

Implications for Leaders and Change Agents

The challenge is no longer to survive but to build pathways to a Preferred Future together and thrive.

Understanding Leadership Today

There has been an incredible amount of research on leadership and even more commentary and interpretation. I want to suggest a simple and basic model: the Lippitt Model of Leadership. It stems from the original and seminal research done in 1945 by Ron Lippitt and Ralph White.[1] Most of the research since then has really built on or been based on this original model. It is still very relevant today and provides us a way to talk about leadership that people from the shop floor to the boardroom can understand and find meaningful. Better than any other model, it takes us to the core issues: control, power, cooperation, and motivation.

Lippitt and White identified three basic styles of leadership: *autocratic, democratic,* and *laissez-faire*. They clearly defined the behaviors and results of each style. What is fascinating to me today, over fifty years later, is that corporate leaders, managers, and supervisors seem to act as if they don't have this knowledge. Debates about the pros and cons of one style or another go on as if people were unaware of what research has shown is the result of these three styles of leadership with regard to productivity, motivation, and the creation of self-directed employees and teams.

The Behaviors of the Three Leadership Styles

In quick review, the autocratic style is defined by the following behaviors:

- Issue the task you want accomplished and the time frame.
- Assert your role is to assure high quality and productivity.
- Direct the activities.
- Appoint roles and responsibilities.
- Establish a work process in which you receive all information and make the decisions.
- Interrupt people if they seem unclear and require specific suggestions.
- Decide on the best solution based on ideas and information.
- Reward obvious high performers.
- Evaluate contributions as good or bad.

The democratic style is defined by the following behaviors:

- Introduce the task and time frame and check for understanding and opinions.
- Explain that your role is to assist everyone to create the best possible product.
- Provide a process for generating and pooling ideas for discussion and decision and ask for other suggestions on how to proceed.
- Make sure all ideas are heard and considered.
- Help timely task achievement by initiating schedule reviews.
- Suggest that others take on responsibility for achieving the task and suggest how this might be done.
- Clarify confusion and misunderstandings in conversations and otherwise facilitate honest and continuous communication throughout.
- Treat people equally and as important.

The laissez-faire style is defined by the following behaviors:

- Ask people if they are ready to begin and ask how they would like to proceed.
- If asked, clarify the task briefly and ask what others think.
- Encourage any and all suggestions.
- Defer to others on all decisions of how to proceed and on best ideas for the product.
- Attempt to clarify confusion and misunderstandings yourself only as a last resort.

The classic research on these three styles identified the typical results of each style—the culture that each created.

The autocratic style produces the following culture:

- Scapegoating, blaming, and aggression in the system
- Apathy
- Domination over others
- Discontent and covert hostility especially toward leaders
- Reliance on authority
- Dependency on the leader for answers and information

The democratic style produces the following culture:

- Full involvement and high amounts of work-oriented conversations
- Willingness to resolve differences between individuals and subgroups
- An efficient balance of taking time for fun and getting things done
- Friendliness and spontaneous cooperation
- Preference for "we" (team) attitude rather than "I" attitude
- Creativity and originality

The laissez-faire style produces the following culture:

- High frustration
- Asking for direction and structure

- Focus on wanting to create structure and direction
- Open discontent and reduced satisfaction
- Communication between people to clarify the task
- Higher orientation on having fun than getting the job done

There is no mistaking these cues and dynamics when one walks into an organization. They are created by how the leadership and membership behave. Over time leadership establishes a clear style and culture throughout the organization.

The Current Leadership Dilemma

I mention this research because, as I said earlier, there is no reason to debate the merits or results of one leadership style over another. The information is here. The question becomes, How do you become the kind of leader you want to be to get the results you want and be consistent with your personal values and beliefs?

Many organizations are shifting their leadership style and culture in the direction of participative or team-based or empowered or employee participation styles. All these, as conceived, fall in the category of the democratic leadership style. Why this shift? More and more leaders are realizing the old top-down system or autocratic style no longer works; it is not cost-effective, nor flexible enough, nor compatible with installing quality, nor consistent with a whole-systems view. And if you pay attention to future trend data, the new workforce is predicted to be much more interested in quality of work life. In a nutshell, they will be interested in more say, not more pay.

I daresay that we are seeing this trend in other parts of the world, indicated by obvious events like the fall of the Berlin Wall. Less obvious events include the work of leaders in other countries to democratize educational systems and encourage greater involvement in economic development activities.

I have worked with many leaders, managers, and supervisors as they try to move from autocratic to democratic styles of leadership, and move to a whole-systems view. Figure 16.1 summarizes the Lippitt Model of Leadership, a model that has helped them understand the task more clearly.

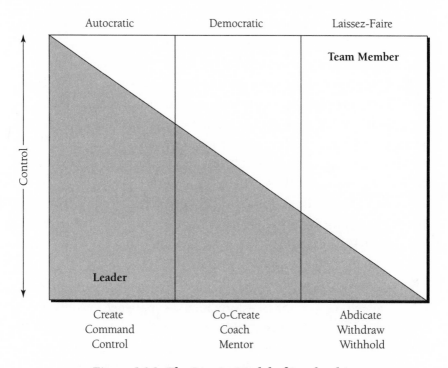

Figure 16.1 The Lippitt Model of Leadership

What leadership characteristics does the model indicate for each style?

• *The authoritarian leader creates.* He or she may create the concept of the new organization or the quarterly goals, or the vision. Command-and-control then becomes the method to get things carried out. Such leaders tend to keep their cards close to their chest. Hidden agendas abound.

• *The democratic leader more actively coaches, mentors, and supports people.* There is much more teaming with stakeholders to co-create such things as key concepts, programs, strategic direction, goals, and new organization structures. People's agendas are more open. Openness of communication and information exchange are valued and practiced. Cooperation increases.

• *The laissez-faire leader withdraws involvement and may even end up withholding useful information.* Such a leader may abdicate responsibility and involvement. Little structure or agenda is provided.

In this model we see that leader control is predominant in the autocratic style. Member control is predominant in the laissez-faire style. And a balance of shared control between leader and members exists in the democratic style. This model contains many degrees of each style. The more one moves from autocratic toward democratic, the more control shifts steadily from predominately leader toward shared between leader and members. Movement from democratic toward laissez-faire shifts the control from being balanced toward higher member control, until ultimately there is anarchy.

What I have seen over and over are two typical traps leaders and managers fall into as they try to move from an autocratic toward a democratic style.

• *Trap #1: Good Intentions, No Follow-Through.* Often, after real soul-searching or some transformational experience, leaders realize that their new style needs to be democratic. So with good intentions they set off to involve and empower people. They make the assumption that since they themselves have made the transformation in consciousness that the rest of the system will have the ability to immediately let go of distrust, many years of wounding from being discounted, and old habits of not telling the truth and getting around the system.

But they find people are unable to easily change, unable to take responsibility without fear, unable to make decisions on their own, and unable to work in self-directed teams. People are, instead, distrustful. At this point it is easy to fall into the trap of getting very frustrated and saying, "See, I knew this stuff wouldn't work anyway!" Or "This is taking too much time and it costs too much!" When they go back to the authoritarian style, then others say, "Yep, I knew it was too good to be true." Or "Another flavor of the month."

• *Trap #2. A Democrat Under Duress.* I have also seen people ordered to not be autocratic any more, but to become democratic (or participative, or team-based, or whatever the phrase of the month happens to be). Typically they don't get any or enough training or coaching to know what that means. But they do have a clear picture, from many years of experience, of what they are not supposed to do. So they try very hard not to be autocratic. Usually this results in them swinging to laissez-faire types of behaviors. What results is frustration on the part of others. Then when a crisis hits or performance goes down and pressure to produce some specific results is applied, such leaders revert to the only thing they know. They become autocratic again to get the job done, making them appear two-faced and insincere. This leaves their direct reports and others feeling confused or double-crossed and angry—and saying, "I knew it, this was too good to last. Nothing has really changed!"

This pattern of swinging from one side to the other side of the extremes, from autocratic to laissez-faire and back, creates a kind of organizational craziness. It is costly to productivity and health. In truth, it would have been better to be a good autocratic leader and open about it.

The leadership dilemma today, then, is how to move toward a more democratic style and avoid the traps along the way. Preferred Futuring provides answers for various levels of leaders.

Changing an Organization's Culture

The Preferred Futuring process is a powerfully effective tool for leaders who want to change the culture of their organization while creating a whole-systems focus on specific business priorities and results. The process is inherently democratic. It provides a methodology for encouraging people to participate fully in a way that taps their passions— their hearts as well as their brains—and overcomes resistance to risk taking and participation with a whole-systems perspective.

Recently I worked with a leadership team of a major testing facility for a U.S. auto maker. They had defined their new core business and designed a new team-based organization structure. The leader decided to initiate a democratic style. It took time for his leadership team to begin to trust his willingness to partner and not have the last word, that it was really one person one vote now on many decisions. We surfaced and helped them recognize their ambivalence, distrust, and resistance to this new style. And they acknowledged their desire for him "to be for real." They wanted to believe that his statement that he couldn't do it without them was genuine. Once this was established as authentic, there was a definite shift in openness and honesty and team member ability to give up old turf ownership so as to redesign a really new organization structure. A kind of healing took place.

Then I asked, "Who else needs to be in the room to discuss the new organization?" They realized they needed to bring in supervisors and technicians who represented different parts of the whole system to test how realistic the new structure was, to help improve it, and then to implement it. So they expanded membership and created a microcosm team of the larger system.

When their expanded team met, the new representatives were skeptical based on their experience; they were fearful of being co-opted or used to sell the new organization to their peers. It took one whole meeting to open up this issue and begin to resolve it. All the years of authoritarian treatment and wounding experiences raised real distrust and resistance.

At the second meeting most new members were able to begin honestly evaluating the core business definition and the new organization structure, and add real value. They began teaming with their superiors to co-create an implementation plan for involving the rest of the organization. The same sense of healing of old wounds that had taken place with the leader and his team was evident again.

Most participants were impressed with these meetings in terms of the effectiveness of the planning process and the quality of the output. But these meetings were about more than just the organization's change in structure and reassessment of their core business. As participants developed trust in each other, they could see the world through the eyes of other parts of the system. They began to understand that installing the new structure was the obvious activity, but it was also a vehicle for deeper leadership style and culture change—it would move leadership from autocratic to democratic throughout the organization. They were gaining a whole-systems perspective.

This was new ground for all of them to be treading. And it was important to recognize that everyone had to discover the new team-based behaviors, not just the official leaders. It now became the job of everyone to help each other to confront old-style behaviors and work them through to keep the culture change going.

Preferred Futuring and the Whole-Systems Leader

The job of leadership needs to be recast in light of how interconnected we are today. It is time for whole-systems leadership. Whole-systems leaders are keepers of the flame. They hold the vision and the faith for the whole system, they enroll others, and they provide heart when it is needed. They understand the power of a common focus on an agreed-upon future that is connected to people's passions. They must help the system hold the focus and proceed with courage. They must continually ask themselves and others, What future do we want? Are we thinking of the whole system? Who needs to be in the room? What does the conversation need to be about?

The Renaissance of a Product Line

In the mid-1980s, I found myself working with a talented engineer in an auto company. He had become one of the nation's brightest experts on Quality Improvement. Currently he was in charge of installing Quality Improvement systems for one of the company's major divisions, comprising several product lines. My colleagues and I were helping him develop and install those systems.

Then it was discovered that the company's prestige product line was running out of warehouse space to hold the rejects and was in serious jeopardy of losing badly to the competition. So he was asked to take the lead engineer position and fix it fast. He took us with him to help do the job.

At this point he was ahead of the rest of his organization, with profound knowledge on Quality Improvement systems and processes, knowledge that the whole organization needed badly but didn't understand or know it needed. His peers in manufacturing engineering, marketing, and finance—and his new boss—were all in this state. Yet immediate results were needed.

Our one-on-one interviews with him and our coaching helped him articulate his vision of the "Excellent Engineering Organization" as it would look if it were operating with high quality as a way of life in everything it did. We wrote this vision down and fed it back for his improvements and pushed him to become even more detailed and to use examples and descriptions of behavior and processes. This became a very powerful and strategic document for that organization—a real competitive advantage if it could be implemented.

This leader was very people-oriented. He demonstrated democratic behavior in his daily activities—to the occasional shock of his peers and managers. For example, he even did away with his executive bathroom and used the public one down the hall. The challenge was to move the vision from his mind to the minds of his leadership team and the rest of the organization . . . and do it now!

We structured a two-day retreat with his team. For the first half day, he presented his vision and answered questions. Often you could hear a pin drop. The forty managers filling the room were stunned, yet somehow given hope by his excitement and commitment and vision. He then said it would only happen if this became their vision also. As we had agreed, he then left the room, leaving instructions that his leadership team was to go through the vision in detail and massage it or change it where they needed to. He would be back in a day to hear their report of the new vision they were willing to subscribe to and make happen. There was no command-and-control, and yet he was certainly not abdicating.

We helped the team wrestle with the vision, make sense of it, and modify it based on their knowledge, and we provided insights into quality-maintenance principles that were relevant. When the leader returned the next afternoon, the team presented their vision. We coached him to be supportive and listen and ask questions, yet not back down on principles or pieces of the vision he felt deeply passionate about. This session ended on an incredible high, with new hope flowing into the leadership team of this organization.

The detailed components of the vision became the source of specific objectives in each year's business plan. And the organization began to align around this vision, as it was carried out to the rest of the organization and translated into daily actions for four years. During this time, the whole system totally redesigned itself, creating new processes that reduced scrap, integrated design and manufacturing engineering, drastically reduced warranty costs, and increased internal customer satisfaction. The product line eventually reclaimed its market share.

When we visited this leader four years later, he expressed some chagrin at not having "paid more attention" to the vision in the fray of turning the organization around. But upon examination, every part and detail of the vision had been implemented. We concluded that these results were due to two things. The vision had been well ingrained in people's thinking as they participated in creating it. And it had been embedded in the yearly business planning cycle. A year later they received the Malcolm Baldrige Award for quality.

Redesigning a State Government Department

The leader of a state government department we have worked with lately was philosophically committed to a team-based, participative, democratic style of leadership and organization culture. Yet he was falling into the trap of moving too far toward laissez-faire. This led at times to various members of the leadership team resorting to an autocratic style to get things done, especially when others below were complaining about wishy-washyness and lack of direction.

At the same time this leader was trying not to be authoritarian, a consultant he hired to work with his leadership team took control of his team and provided a vision for them. The leader became fearful that if he challenged this so-called expert he might lose his team, which was quite enamored of the consultant. This created a very large crisis for this leader. He had many very innovative and participative ideas, but was not able to adequately express them and ironically was fearful to express them to his organization. When the consultant lost favor and was not rehired, however, an opening for action was created.

In a coaching context, I asked the leader about the organization he saw in the future, the organization that excited and pleased him. My partner and I took notes as I pushed him to be specific, and after we wrote these notes up into a detailed vision statement, he began using them to communicate his views and ideas more clearly.

He could then talk to his leadership team about what it would mean to be a leader in the new organization they were creating. This required them to define the new leadership style so it could be communicated, necessary training could be developed, and hiring and evaluation criteria could be made consistent with this new definition. A microcosm team (representative of the whole system) was established to develop this new model, and the new leadership model was successfully implemented.

This has been a major redesign event for a government department that had not changed since anyone could remember. The organization is now more responsive to customers and has reduced by 25 percent the number of employees required to get the job done.

A New Organization Model for the Future

It has become very clear that we have been stuck for too long with the pyramidal top-down model. People are searching for a new way to express our organization structure and charts. Some have turned the pyramid upside down. That makes a certain point, but does not offer a new model.

Most of the current models of organization focus on structure; some include processes as well. Many seem to leave out key elements such as values and beliefs or myths or feelings or basic human needs. These elements, however, must be in any true organizational model because every organization is a human system. Certainly any model for the '90s and beyond needs to include these dimensions of human systems. I propose a model, shown in Figure 16.2, which incorporates the aspects of a human system: The Organization Tree of Life.[2]

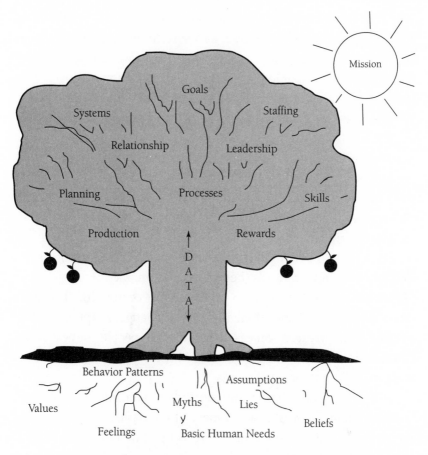

Figure 16.2 The Organization Tree of Life Model

The metaphor is that an organization is like a tree, a living, breathing, growing system, sensitive to and interdependent with the environment. The obvious part is above the ground. Most models focus on this part and include components like leadership, structures, planning, production, work processes, staffing and development, compensation and rewards. In our model the vision and mission are metaphorically represented as the sun because they provide the context and vital energy without which the system does not grow and produce the fruits of its labor such as products or services. Some models also include this component. But there is much more below ground.

Like trees, organizations have an extensive underground component or root system. The tree, as a system, is equally as large and extensive below the ground as it is above the ground. Human organizations are the same. Most organization models don't recognize this extensive subsurface portion of their structure. But human systems, just like trees, are dependent upon this lower portion and will sicken and die if it isn't working.

The below-ground portion of an organization is made up of patterns of behavior, values, myths, beliefs about people and organizations and work, underlying assumptions—the individual feelings and the socioemotional climate, the little white lies we tell ourselves and the basic human needs we all have. These are present in any human system. A key to system performance (above ground) becomes how well the basic human needs (below ground) are met.

Whether the basic human needs are met or not often becomes a root cause for an organization's inability to change, adapt, or perform well and maximize its resources. When we help people connect around their passions and include their view of the system in the vision, we are tapping into these basic needs.

There is a set of basic human needs universally present in any human system. This list is a summary of the basic human needs recognized across most schools or theories of psychology.[3] Most psychologists would agree that people feel good about themselves and others with whom they associate—and function harmoniously, cooperatively, and productively—when they feel:

- Liked and respected
- Accepted
- Useful
- Included
- Influential
- Considered
- Growing in skill and autonomy
- Positively interrelated with those they live and work with
- A sense of adventure
- A part of and belonging to something larger than self

The results are predictable and consistent when one or more of these needs are not met and people don't feel this way about themselves. They often behave in so-called negative ways in order to regain a sense of feeling important and in control. They may try to get attention by behaving annoyingly or charmingly, by being clinging and dependent or irrelevant or silly. Some may try to get revenge for feeling neglected or for being put down. Some may dominate the situation by bossing and trying to be the one in control. Some may just retreat and become completely passive while others may engage in sabotage.

When these behaviors occur in a human system, it is probably not an indication of a bad person or some character flaw. It is a symptom, a warning that some basic human needs are not being met in the system. To follow the tree analogy further, the basic human needs could be likened to root hairs that draw life-giving energy in the form of water and nutrients from the ground, which sustain life. Without healthy root hairs, the tree can become diseased, struggle for existence, and eventually die.

This new organization model provides a basis for more completely understanding organizations as whole systems. It is a way to more completely diagnose root causes for organizational systems and processes that are not working. But most important, it provides a more complete vision of a Preferred Future for our organization as a whole system. The implication: As we create a vision of our organization's future, we must include these aspects of organizational life; the dimensions that are below the ground in the Organization Tree of Life Model are the keys to success.

Conclusion

As leaders and change agents it is our job to help create pathways to the future. So my thesis is really that if we can find a way to help people think of their whole system, ask people about the future they want, listen to them, and find ways to record it, then we can begin to create an exciting Preferred Future. This moves hopes and intentions to acts of creation. Preferred Futuring is a very useful and powerful tool for conscious, planned, and transformational organization redesign. It can help people empower themselves. This is basic to success!

Unless we do this, people will be less likely to create the kind of system they really want. We must open up the window and expand the field of vision for people as they invent the new organizations. This is leadership for the '90s and beyond.

Why Preferred Futuring Really Works: The Scientific and Spiritual Basis

The truth is that thinking in the future tense from a perspective of clarity about what I want becomes an act of creation in the present.

Looking to the Future, Not the Past

Why does Preferred Futuring work? Knowing this will allow you to use this powerful tool even more effectively.

For some time it has been obvious to those of us who use it that Preferred Futuring is a powerful way to mobilize and focus the human energy of any system. Deep and lasting change with transformative results occurs. When people's hearts and minds converge, we begin working at a deeper or soul level of the organization. People let go and allow something greater to emerge for the whole system. It often feels like we are all walking on the edge of chaos together and this is our collective laboratory as we learn how to create a new future reality. But why does this happen?

When a group of people—any system—focuses with passion and commitment on a common vision, not only is enormous energy created, but this field of energy is generative—energy producing more energy and concrete results. It is also regenerative—healing old wounds so that people and organizations can move forward. Thus understanding why

Preferred Futuring works involves another paradigm shift: how we see cause and effect.

The Scientific Basis for Preferred Futuring

For a long time our understanding of cause and effect has been based on the Newtonian physics model, postulating that the past causes the present. Metaphorically, causes occur from collisions like those where one billiard ball bumps into another, bumping into another, and so on. It is a linear, mechanical model suggesting that causes lead to effects. In Newtonian physics there is room only for change though collision and conflict, through the energy of bumping into and making something more, through *fission.*

This view is being replaced increasingly by the quantum physics notion that the anticipated effects are in fact the cause—our presence modifies the event. The effects of the envisioned future (expectations) cause the present (actions). Quantum physics is a model of receiving, of absorbing. When a collision happens, the energy is absorbed by both, and something more is made through *fusion.*

This paradigm shift includes movement away from the Cartesian philosophy, which suggests that everything runs on logic and reason. Since the Renaissance, logic and reason have ruled supreme. This is being gently and often quietly replaced by a new whole system of philosophy that is both scientific and spiritual. This philosophy is based on imagination and creativity, yet includes logic and reason.

Creating Reality

Each of us is creating reality at every moment and have been since we began. There are now many authors describing this phenomenon. Deepak Chopra, in *Quantum Healing* and other books, has documented how focusing the mind can cause or heal physical illness.[1] He finds that focus and belief are key. Michael Talbot, in his book, *The Holographic Universe,* documents this phenomenon.[2] There are a growing number of books instructing us about how to affirm and focus on the reality we want. Twenty years ago Robert Rosenthal discovered what was called the self-fulfilling prophecy phenomenon and described it in *Pygmalion in the Classroom.*[3] How we think and behave toward a person determines how they perform and behave in the classroom, the family, or the workplace. We are now discovering that how we see ourselves and how others see us influence the creation of our reality and the future.

Quantum physicists have shown that reality is energy and matter in constant flux. Chopra and others have shown that thought can direct and focus energy, and we create reality by what we focus our thoughts upon and therefore focus our energy upon.

That we create reality is not such a leap of faith any more. This leaves us in a very exciting place. We can create reality by worrying and get what we don't want, or create reality by Preferred Futuring and get what we do want. The choice becomes ours! Using a whole-systems view and generating our collective Preferred Future is a total-systems act of creation.

The act of identifying the future we prefer becomes simultaneously an act of creation and a quest. As soon as we decide on a future we want and move to achieve it, we learn. Thus we become capable of creating an even more exciting and more deeply meaningful future reality. This becomes a cycle of transformation and positive change.

So Preferred Futuring is about creating reality. If we think, it begins to become real. And continued focus and action make it become so. Yet it is natural to experience resistance to change, including this change. To continue the conscious creation process, we must recognize the beliefs that can limit the future for successful action taking, and let them go. So in order to create a new or expanded reality one must make room by letting go of the current one, including certain beliefs and memories.

Splitting the Human Energy Atom

I use the metaphor of "splitting the human energy atom" because to our Newtonian minds it connotes awesome release of energy. Opening up to and declaring the future we really want does that. It is really a quantum process of allowing growth, expansion, absorption, and focus of energy. Fusion, not fission. The power of focusing on the future has become obvious over the years and is still unfolding with the writing of this book and our current work in whole systems.

The story of this discovery includes my search for new and expanded ways of helping people to be empowered and successful in their lives and organizations, and to bring deeper meaning to our own lives and the lives of others. During fifteen years in Vajrayana Buddhist (Tibetan) training, I was led to an interest in more holistic approaches to healing and change. I learned methodologies that focus and work with the energy centers and energy fields of the body, mind, and spirit. And I was stunned by the results.

As one directs energy through portions of a client's body to release stored-up emotional blocks, the client's immediate reactions are noticeable. The client's increased capabilities seem very tangible. This has led me to respect deeply and more richly understand what "focusing our energy" can really mean at an individual and large system level.

This is consistent with my observations on being a whole-systems change agent. When people work together with the same picture of success, that picture is more likely to happen. But something else is going on when we do whole-systems futuring sessions and the usual helpful things to facilitate action. At a whole other energy level, a group of people is focusing its hopes, thoughts, and beliefs toward the same picture of a future reality. I have felt and seen the power of this, and have experienced goose bumps at key points in work with large client groups, and now more fully understand what is going on. I suspect that whole organizations have their own energy fields, much like each of us do.

What we have begun to realize is that we were simultaneously working at the organizational quantum level of creating a new reality as well. This is why, when the picture and belief is so clear and pure, it seems that things just happen as if the universe is cooperating. It isn't just serendipity. It has to do with the collective conviction that this is right and possible. Literally this directed energy field creates form, and it creates healing and wholeness.

Healing the Human Spirit at the Organization Level

While working with some supervisors and middle managers in a plant, I found myself listening differently to their accounts of experiences that supported the notion that nothing could or would be done. It was not very different from other moments in other groups we try to help become empowered. They were telling their stories of being treated as if their opinions and ideas weren't valuable even though they were capable and creative people. But in this situation, I stopped understanding this as normal resistance that happens when upper levels decide to empower people they regard as theirs after years of disempowerment. All at once I saw them as very wounded (abused in a sense) people. This woundedness went back many years in most cases. Their human spirit had been broken or fragmented. They needed to become whole again. They needed healing of some kind before they could be empowered. This is the case in many of the companies where we work.

This perspective helped me openly confront these supervisors about their defeatist attitude: I acknowledged my own sense of hopelessness as I listened to them and pointed out the choice to not go on. This led to a real breakthrough with one member who had been keeping his woundedness and resistance hidden. He blew up, and years of frustration poured out. But afterward, he realized that keeping these feelings in was preventing him from moving on, from making a conscious decision to try to make things better.

The group then decided to take the risk, act as if they were empowered, and execute the action plans to involve employees in a self-managed process. Some healing had taken place for this one individual and for the whole group. More healing would occur as the team successfully acted on a vision of an empowered organization. This process will need to be repeated numerous times to make the plan work and the vision become manifest throughout.

The Power of Healing

It is exciting to think about the power this awareness can give us all. The real job is not process improvement or redesign or even empowerment of self-directed teams. These are just methodologies. The real task before us is to heal and make whole again. Accomplishing the deeper healing makes the other stuff of process improvement or re-design easier and more likely to work. Creating a shared vision quickly brings resistances to the surface. Then working through the resistances brings about the necessary healing and becoming whole, for the organization and for both individual leaders and workers. This has been happening all along for our clients where we have used the Preferred Futuring methodology. Now I understand it more deeply and completely—it explains why Preferred Futuring works and why it is such a powerful tool. This leads me to propose a new model for change.[4]

The Quantum Change Model

Figure 17.1 shows the new Quantum Change Model, which helps us understand and focus our work at the soul or transformational level for healing and change. The model works for any system; individual, group, organization or community.

At any present point of reality (shown as Δ in Figure 17.1), we can look back and identify the events that have led us to that point and assume the next logical future choice "e" is directly ahead. This is illustrated by the statement, "Well, it has always been this way and so it will be in the future." This is the Newtonian assumption.

Or we can energize and empower another future state ("a" through "d" or "f" through "i"), illustrated by the statement, "Any future scenario is possible and I prefer this one ('b' for example)." The task of creation becomes that of choosing from any number of possible future realities arrayed out there and energizing our choice, being pulled by it and directing our energies into it. At any present moment, we can change from potential future "e" to another potential future, "b" for example. This is the Quantum assumption.

I have come to believe that both Quantum and Newtonian principles work. It is not a matter of which is right. They both are. The question is which one to use to create reality. Quantum principles create more breakthrough or transformative results and are more rapid.

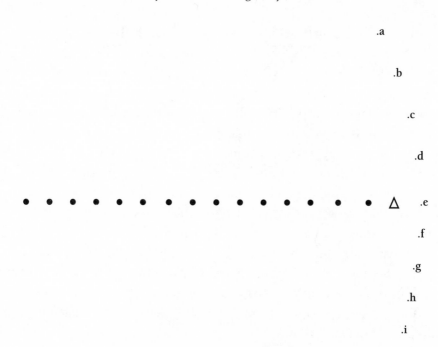

Figure 17.1 The Quantum Change Model

It is becoming more attractive to work with clients and choose friends who are also open to working consciously at the quantum level in their lives and their organizations, rather than at the Newtonian level. It is very much like Sanaya Roman's wonderful book *Living with Joy*.[5] She points out that we have the choice to choose the path of pain or joy as we move through this life and learn what we are to learn. Put that way, if "b" is the path of joy, why not make the transformative shift! The answer, of course, raises all the resistant beliefs: "it has to hurt to learn," "it has always been painful and embarrassing so it will never be joyful to learn and grow," "you don't deserve joy," and so on. This is what I call the Quantum Choice Point where we can let go of the past and operate from imagination and not memory. Operate from our Preferred Future and not our fears or worries or disappointments. What we need is a picture of the future that we want—that excites us and sings the song of our soul.

The Spiritual Basis of Preferred Futuring

As people reach new levels of honesty by sharing their different views of what is going on (the current state), core beliefs, and vision of a future that lights their passions, this builds an energy field around the organization and community that allows Preferred Futuring to take place. This energy field, as it continues to be built, generates the future state. This startling awareness seems to match the electricity that one feels in the room, in the organization, or in the town where we facilitate Preferred Futuring. It helps to explain the deep and transformative change that results in these human systems. As change agents we must understand how to catalyze and help build these energy fields. We need to understand more deeply how energy works. Not only is there a scientific explanation, there is a spiritual explanation that helps to deepen our understanding of Preferred Futuring and how to use it more effectively.

Besides the scientific paradigm shift that I mentioned earlier, there is spiritual paradigm shift as well. I began to be aware of it in the late 1970s when I read an article in a popular psychology magazine that talked about the presence of "psychic healing" groups meeting in suburban living rooms. It seems that people were pursuing spiritual and holistic avenues, but no one talked about it. This caused the misconception that no one else was interested, while people were secretly gathering to explore these avenues in living rooms all across the country.

Although there is still hesitancy to acknowledge this in most organizations and workplaces in the 1990s, the revolution is more openly upon us. We see *New York Times* Best Seller List books dealing with caring for the soul or applying spiritual principles to business and leadership, and quantum physics writers discussing the nature of the soul.[6]

Spirit and Work: The Top Line and the Bottom Line

In the 1970s those of us who were organization development consultants and change agents carried the torch for humanizing the workplace. During this time many business leaders reminded consultants that the bottom line was also very important. Without it no one has a workplace, humanistic or not. Both leaders in industry and consultants grew through this interaction. Now we are facing another such evolutionary event. In addition to the bottom line, we must now also attend to what I call the *top line*. By top line I refer to the rapidly increasing focus on spirit and Soul, or the higher self, in the work place.

Today bringing spirit into our lives and into the workplace is becoming more popular and even fashionable, and certainly important. This is probably our next evolutionary step—to realize that the teachings of great spiritual leaders has relevancy for daily behavior on the job or off the job. The very popular Stephen Covey books (for example) are really a translation of basic Mormon spiritual principles into everyday business terms.[7]

I have taken the time to observe my own journey. I have also had the honor to be part of the journeys of many others in the context of managing change in our lives and organizations, always trying to capture the deeper meaning of what is going on in the situation. It is increasingly clear to me that acknowledging the spiritual component of a situation increases the depth of our understanding.

Discovering That the Real Reality Is the Internal One

Many spiritual traditions that are hundreds of years old, as well as quantum physics and some current new spiritual approaches that are emerging, all suggest the same point: our external reality is merely a reflection of our internal reality. Thus our external reality is a reflection of our beliefs about what we deserve as well as what we can imagine and declare that we want and believe we can have.

In 1994 I heard a speech by the Dalai Lama, exiled political leader of Tibet, spiritual leader of the Tibetan Buddhist religion worldwide, and Nobel Peace prize recipient. To an entire sports arena of local citizens and members of the University of Michigan academic community, he gave some sage advice on developing the ability to think in terms of the whole system. He was humble and his message simple. Develop our hearts as well as our minds and realize that world peace is ultimately crucial, and that peace out in the world begins with working for peace within ourselves.

He then went on to point out that it is easier to be loving and compassionate and peaceful inside and project it outward when things are going well. Our increased spiritual strength and growth comes, he said, from being loving and compassionate and continuing to create a positive and peaceful reality when we feel in opposition and it does not seem like an easy situation.

Since our external reality reflects our beliefs, we change out there by changing in here. We must change the internal landscape to manifest physical reality out there. Our beliefs and sense of what we really deserve or can have are too often very real limits on the reality we can create. This implies that our work as whole-systems preferred futurers and change agents involves some aspects of our individual and collective inner healing as well.

The most profound healing or transformation comes from the realization that the resistances are always in us, not out there. Identifying and letting go of our own resistance, our own attachments to memories and limiting beliefs, is the ultimate key. Of course, helping others to do this becomes part of our job as agents of change, leaders, and preferred futurers.

Alone we can create our realities. But together we can do much more—and do it much better and much quicker. The ability to help everyone focus on the same desired future creates something exponentially more powerful. This is the power and payoff of whole-systems Preferred Futuring and the various methodologies that have sprung from it.

I believe a key contextual shift is happening, and is even a part of whole-systems thinking. There is a point when one realizes that spiritual work *is* the work. Behaving according to a set of spiritual principles at work is our real work as well. It becomes important to be alive with and aware of spirit in everything we do and embody that in our project or staff or board meetings. What follows are four basic principles to guide our journey as we create the future we prefer, which includes deeper meaning in our lives and organizations.

- *Principle 1. We are spirit.* I believe that we are not just physical beings having an occasional spiritual experience. In fact we are spiritual beings as well. Each spiritual tradition, in one way or another, recognizes that we are all "children of God" or "Children of Allah" or "Boddhisatvas" or have in us "the divine Spark." The message has been consistently there for centuries. I believe we are all a part of the divine; an individual expression of the divine . . . a soul. It is as if the divine is the ocean and a soul is created by dipping into that ocean with a cup. That cupful of the divine becomes an individual expression of spirit, a soul such as you or me.

Since we spend much of our active time at work, why not act out of who we really are at work as well? The key challenge then becomes remembering who we are and operating out of spiritual principles of love and compassion rather than fear and competitiveness.

Each great religion probes the question, Why am I here? It is entirely possible that our purpose as a soul is to learn and grow spiritually through becoming involved in our physical existence. Possibly we are here for a time in the work of individuals, groups, and organizations and nations to learn; this is our classroom. But it is easy to lose track of this core purpose of spiritual growth and learning. As we become involved in our physical existence, as we strive to meet quarterly objectives, get that raise, and so on, these become paramount instead. We lose track of what we really want: to live in a state of love and grace and joy and engage in relationships and activities that have deeper meaning. We lose track of who we are and why we are here.

It is important to shift our focus back to recognizing we are spiritual beings—souls, with a physical body for a period of time to learn and grow as a soul and offer certain gifts that we have while we are here. The supervisors in the example cited earlier in this chapter may have seemed a long way from this point of view, but we can begin to see that this was their ultimate destination. Human spiritual growth and evolution toward wholeness happens in organization settings just as much as other arenas of life. We just have to drop some of our beliefs that it is not appropriate or possible at work, or that no one else would consider this possibility with us. Work is a large part of our classroom, and a potential source of learning.

Compared to our working alone, Preferred Futuring can bring us closer to who we are or can be, and it can bring us there more quickly and at a more profound level as a connected unity of individuals. Done right, Preferred Futuring pulls from people's souls to create the future. In contrast, a focus on problems or fear or being in control pulls from our egos rather than from our souls. Preferred Futuring helps us to raise up the core resistances and fears in a way that makes deep or soul-level transformations more likely than any other process I have seen. The question becomes whether the change agent and the system are ready, skilled enough, and willing to enter into real soul-level healing and transformational change. It requires a partner relationship between system and change agent and a willingness to take a journey together.

• *Principle 2. We are all connected.* A poet once said that you can't pick a flower but that you shake the most distant star. And quantum physicists as well as Eastern spiritual leaders have told us that everything in the universe is connected. It is reported that Jesus said, "Do unto others as you would have others do unto you," and that the Buddha said, "What you do to others, you also do to yourself." So this idea that all things are interconnected is not a new notion. In fact none of these principles that help us operate from our soul or higher self are new.

We are now coming closer to this principle in the workplace with the current interest in systems thinking. In the automotive industry, for example, we are learning to focus on not just the parts and subsystems but the whole vehicle. Many companies are learning the importance of moving beyond the notions of departmental turf or organizational chimneys. Cross-system collaboration and partnering is becoming essential and more frequently used. People now see that what one department does affects other departments. When we operate solely out of our subsystem worlds, we lose effectiveness as a larger system. People are becoming more interested in the skills of collaboration and working as a team.

The irony of this is that while we are all connected, we don't seem to focus on or even realize this, and there is a growing sense in organizations of a need to be connected or feel connected at work. A loss of a job is not just about income and house and car, it is about loss of connection with people. The further irony is that people often go around undermining this connection they desperately want. They do this by acting out of fear and not being open and honest with each other. We do things that separate us and shatter our ability to feel connected.

• *Principle 3. We exist in an energy field that we create.* Vision and intention create reality. The Quantum Change Model described earlier illustrates the basic principle.

Simply put, we can create a reality that is an extension of our past, or we can change our beliefs and intentions and create a trans- formative future reality. What gives rise to our beliefs and intentions is the future. It can be the one we want or the one we don't want. It is up to us and depends on having a clear vision, intentions, beliefs, and trust.

I have seen many organizations and individuals struggle with managing change that seems chaotic. To create a detailed picture of the future of choice, more than any other single act, reduces the fearful feeling of chaos, tends to bring focus, clarity, and constancy of pur- pose, and helps achieve the desired results.

• *Principle 4. Health means wholeness.* Two things have convinced me that healing is necessary as part of change and transformation in systems: the prevalence of resistance and the effect of healing.

The phenomenon of resistance comes up once an exciting and breakthrough Preferred Future has been envisioned. Resistance creates behaviors very much like the attitudes, voices, and words of deep help- lessness associated with abusive relationships. I wondered about this. Then it made sense when I realized that people have been in top-down systems for ten, twenty, or more years, relationships in which they were told fairly consistently that they were incapable of making key deci- sions or acting as responsible and intelligent adults capable of running their part of the workplace. This has had an impact similar to that of long-term abuse.

We will sometimes find a team or staff so wounded that they see no reason for developing a Preferred Future vision, because it will just get changed by those with more power in the system later. So why bother?

The effect of healing also validates the necessity for healing. And from a macro point of view, developing more participative structures and using more participative methods such as Preferred Futuring is having a collective healing effect on the workplace. Leaders, organizations, all of us have an opportunity to help this spiritual and psychological healing happen at work. If healing is not included as part of the redesign and change management process in organizations, resistance will continue and we will become less and less productive, or change will continue to take longer than necessary and be more costly than necessary.

A New Organizational Model

Historically, the pyramid model of organization structure was developed to cope with crowding, as villages became cities and the task of administration became more complex. Until recently, it has been the only model we have known. George Land suggests that the invention of the hierarchical structure for organizing civic and then industrial systems was a major "break point" from the structures in use by tribes.[8] He has pointed out that we are developmentally at the next break point as a species. This is evidenced by a growing interest in cooperation, collaborative processes, and teaming. We are moving to a new paradigm of relationship at work. There will be more partnering between what has been known as management and workers. The new model will be about co-creation: creating new knowledge and products and structures and processes together, rather than one person or elite group creating while the rest just implement.

When we are talking about building team-based organizations, we are talking about organizing to co-create, partner, and share technology, responsibility, and decision making. Co-creation is where we are going. We are currently inventing what the next organizational model will look like.

This next organizational model involves the "heart connection." People are excited about dialogue now because it helps to look at underlying assumptions and get to deeper meanings of work issues and new possibilities. It helps people break from the constant focus on decision making and deliverables, and take time to look deeper and discover more profound issues. Learning to operate from the heart is more acceptable today. Leading from the heart is now the title of a book.[9]

I would suggest learning to listen from the heart as a first step. Usually we listen from our head, cognitively. This often results in more separation between people. It is a profound experience to listen from the heart. The heart is the window to the soul. We can connect as souls in the workplace this way. It also leads to kinder and more caring attitudes, greater trust, and greater ability to collaborate. As we work collectively at the level of the organizational soul, it may mean moving beyond "learning organizations" to "caring organizations." When we listen from a whole-systems point of view, we are present and see the world through the other person's window on reality. This is a good start.

When operating from the heart, people notice a gentle power. It is a shift from aggressive or pushy power to a presence that grows. In the context of the workplace, it seems linked to relating as a spiritual being who affects both the bottom line and the top line positively.

These four principles are key to leading organizations through change and developing pathways to the future—to change human systems, our organizations, institutions, and communities, and help them become whole.

You Have to Mean It

Good luck. This book has what you need to use Preferred Futuring in your organization or situation for whole-systems change. But please, don't use Preferred Futuring if you want to maintain and strengthen a hierarchical organization; it won't work. Preferred Futuring is very powerful and can focus the energy of a whole system. But don't use the process unless you are willing to empower others to become part of the process and participate in determining the outcomes. If you believe that you have all the answers, it won't work. If you believe the answers are in the whole system, it will work. You have to mean it.

Let's Network

We are glad to share more successes and new learnings with you in the future. If you tell us your successes and learnings we will share ours with you. You can contact us at lippitt@bizserve.com.

Appendix A

Reality Checklist

Need

1. To what extent does this planned change effort relate to our mission and Preferred Future?

   | Is not related | 1 | 2 | 3 | 4 | 5 | Highly related |

2. Is it needed?

   | No need | 1 | 2 | 3 | 4 | 5 | Urgent need |

3. Do you perceive that this need is felt by others who would be involved?

   | Not felt | 1 | 2 | 3 | 4 | 5 | Strongly felt |

4. Does it duplicate any present programs?

   | High duplication | 1 | 2 | 3 | 4 | 5 | No duplication |

Information

5. Do we understand the change effort well enough to explain it to others?

   | Don't understand | 1 | 2 | 3 | 4 | 5 | Fully understand |

Circumstances

6. Are there any unusual circumstances that might prevent us from starting (changes in leadership, funding, participants, and so on)?

| Very unusual | 1 | 2 | 3 | 4 | 5 | None that I know |

7. Are any changes foreseen that could help us get it started?

| None that I know | 1 | 2 | 3 | 4 | 5 | Very possibly |

Timing

8. How flexible is our implementation schedule?

| Schedule is full | 1 | 2 | 3 | 4 | 5 | Still flexible |

9. Are we looking at the best time to introduce the change?

| Worst possible | 1 | 2 | 3 | 4 | 5 | Excellent |

Ability

10. Is cost a problem?

| Great problem | 1 | 2 | 3 | 4 | 5 | No problem |

11. Is the time demand realistic?

| Excessive | 1 | 2 | 3 | 4 | 5 | OK |

12. Can we recruit capable leaders?

| Great difficulty | 1 | 2 | 3 | 4 | 5 | No difficulty |

Values

13. Is the planned change in conflict with our organization's philosophy and style?

| Serious conflict | 1 | 2 | 3 | 4 | 5 | No conflict |

14. How comfortable are you with the philosophy and approach?

Feel						Can
uneasy	1	2	3	4	5	support it

15. Do you believe that "the powers that be" really support the philosophy or approach?

Very						Very
unlikely	1	2	3	4	5	likely

Resistances

16. Will some people have a strong negative reaction to it?

Expect strong negative reaction						Expect strong positive reaction
	1	2	3	4	5	

17. Will some people say they are too busy to participate?

Most will	1	2	3	4	5	Few will

18. Will people be suspicious of why we are introducing the change?

Strong suspicion						No suspicion
	1	2	3	4	5	

19. Are you concerned that this program will add to your workload?

Very concerned						Not concerned
	1	2	3	4	5	

20. How do you feel about the changes it would bring to your area of responsibility?

Reluctant	1	2	3	4	5	Eager

Yield

21. Is the planned change likely to work?

Convinced it won't						Convinced it will
	1	2	3	4	5	

22. Will the payoff be worth the effort?

No	1	2	3	4	5	Yes

Appendix B

Task Force Summary Report

1. Task force action goal: _____

   _____

2. Recorder: _____ Phone: (Day) _____ (Night) _____

3. Names of task force members (List on back of sheet) _____

4. Convener of next meeting: _____

5. Next meeting: (Place) _____ (Date) _____ (Time) _____

6. The next steps of start-up action we are considering are: ____

   _____

7. WHO will do WHAT before the next meeting (for example, invite others, get information)? _____

8. What will be agenda topics for the next meeting? _____

   _____

9. What kind of help, if any, do you need from the steering committee? Or what suggestions do you have for them? _____

   _____

IMPORTANT: Be sure this form includes your task force members' names, addresses, phone and fax numbers, and e-mail addresses.

Appendix C

Preferred Futuring Event Agenda for an Organization or Institution

Day 1 (Participants are in table groups)

Time	Activities
8:30	Welcome (by the CEO)
9:10	Purpose and outcomes of event (by design team members)
9:20	Statement of corporate leadership commitment (by the CEO)
9:30	Context for the event, agenda and ground rules (by consultant and design team)
9:50	Table introductions
	A. Name and responsibility
	B. What I need to get out of these two days to make it worthwhile
10:20	Team-building exercise conducted by facilitators: Explain diversity in the room and its importance in working as a team
	A Strengths we offer
	B. What we need from others
2:00	Lunch
1:30	Historical Review: How we got to where we are today—a time line presentation by the design team
1:50	Our Mission and Vision

A. Orientation
    1. What a mission and a vision are
    2. How do you develop them, what you do with them, and will they be there in the morning?
    3. The process for involvement and participation in the process
B. Leadership team presentation
    1. What business are we in?
    2. Who are our customers?
    3. What are their needs and expectations?
    4. Their view of mission and vision

3:30 Participants React to Mission and Vision Presentation
A. What did we hear—our questions of understanding?
B. Is leaders' mission and vision complete? Is it accurate?
C. Do we agree with it? Can we add value?

4:00 Prouds and Sorries (table groups)
A. List Prouds and Sorries and choose top three of each
B. Report out and capture common themes

5:00 Review agenda for tonight

5:30 Supper

7:30 Revised Mission Presented by Leadership Team
A. Table groups discuss "Did they get it?"
B. Table groups report out

8:00 Values and Beliefs (table groups)
A. Values that have driven us in the past, good and bad
B. Core values that will drive us in the future

9:00 Discuss agenda for tomorrow
Evaluations of day's work

Day 2 (Table groups until 11:25 A.M., functional groups thereafter)

Time   *Activities*

8:45 Facilitators present the whole-systems futuring model
A. Steps in the process
B. The Change Model (discussed in Chapter Fourteen)

9:10	Events, Trends, and Developments (presented by facilitator)
9:45	Our Preferred Future Vision
	A. Presentation of corporate leadership team vision (their set of images)
	B. Table groups build on or modify based on what we see in our preferred future that excites us
10:10	C. Create Preferred Future Vision (paper, markers, glue sticks given; participants work in table groups)
	1. Participants describe the future that excites them
	2. They post items in original categories or create a new one
10:45	3. They vote on visions and break
11:25	Reality check of the vision with the mission
	A. Functional groups combine new material with leadership vision and agree on vision
	B. Groups discuss implications and action ideas
12:00	Lunch
1:00	C. Functional groups continue work
1:45	D. Functional group reports (two minutes each)
2:15	Action Goals
	A. Executive team reports on intended actions and next steps in each area
2:45	B. Table groups add value to action steps and discuss their roles and responsibilities for follow up
4:15	Action Plan: First steps and who is accountable
	A. Functional teams discuss and decide
5:00	B. Quick reports about first steps
5:30	Supper
7:30	Creating Implementation Structure
	A. Presented by executive team
	B. Max-mix table groups (heterogeneous groups) discuss "what I think I heard and our added value."
8:30	Next Steps
9:00	Wrap-up and meeting evaluation

Appendix D

Agenda for Volunteer Training Session

Co-Convener Orientation

Co-Convener Role

Your job is to co-lead a futuring session in which you will gather information vital to determining the future of the community from everyone who attends the session(s).

Co-Convener Skills

Simply welcome people, listen to and accept their ideas, try to answer questions as simply as possible or promise to find an answer and phone them back, and run the meeting in a relaxed yet focused manner.

We know that your fellow citizens—participants in the group(s) that you lead—will have a worthwhile and exciting experience because of your help.

The Coordinating Committee promises to do a careful job of collating and using the data created in your session, and we invite you to take on a special role in the (name of the city or county) "Choosing Our Future" conference.

Plan for Your Meeting

Pre-meeting   Arrive early and arrange chairs and tables, arrange a sign-in sheet and name tags in a convenient place, and arrange any refreshments that you plan to provide.

Meeting Start-Up   The idea is that the session starts for everyone as soon as they walk in the door. As they enter ask them to:

1. Sign the sign-in sheet.
2. Make a name tag from a 3"×5" card by writing their name in good size print with a felt tip pen.
3. Complete the following two thoughts on the sign-in sheet below their names:

   My best experience of living in the (name of city or county) area . . .   _____

   My most frustrating experience of living in the (name of city or county) area . . . _____
4. Get involved in conversation about their experiences at their assigned tables.

Convene the session no more than ten to fifteen minutes after the announced starting time.

The Meeting

(10 min.)   1. Start the meeting with a statement about why you are there (play a tape or read a statement or use your own words). Introduce the co-convener's and your own responsibilities.

2. Verify that everyone is signed in. State the estimated length of the meeting (from fifty minutes to one-and-one-half hours) depending on your specific plan.

(5 min.)   3. Use a warm-up activity about current trends to get the participants thinking about issues that may affect their quality of life in the future. Start with some examples such as rising housing costs, life-long education, and changing demographics. Ask participants to call out other issues while you list them on a flip chart.

(10 min.) 4. List Prouds and Sorries about the (name of city or county). Give an example and ask participants at each table to record as many as they can on the paper you have provided. Then ask them to go back and list the three proudest Prouds and three sorriest Sorries.

(5 min.) 5. Ask participants to call out examples of their proudest Prouds and sorriest Sorries, and collect lists.

(10 min.) 6. Introduce and take the future trip. Ask participants to jump ahead in time to five to ten years in the future. Ask them to imagine that they are on this journey together, looking down on the whole city (county) area with perfect vision. They can see and hear what people are saying and doing and deciding. Ask participants to list what really pleases them about what has happened since the futuring process began back in (current date). Have them write clearly and legibly.

(10 min.) 7. Post table lists and have everyone vote for the ten most exciting images by marking a checkmark or dot next to their selections.

(10 min.) 8. Select the item with the most votes and have everyone brainstorm about all the things that might be done to move toward this goal. Have the co-conveners record the ideas on a central list at the front of the room.

(5 min.) 9. Evaluate the meeting by asking participants to complete one of the following thoughts:

My feelings about the (city or county) area futuring effort are . . . _____

_____

My feelings about this session are . . . _____

_____

My hopes for the (city or county) area Futures project are . . . _____

_____

(5 min.)   10. Provide a volunteer sign-up sheet at the door and request that participants sign it if they want to get more
involved in helping with the futuring effort. And thank
participants for coming.

Post-meeting   After the meeting, package up the information generated by the group and return it to the Futuring office.

Notes

Introduction

1. This section is based on unpublished remarks by Ed Lindaman about thinking in the future tense.
2. As reported to Ron Lippitt by Ed Lindaman and recorded in the private papers of Ron Lippitt.
3. Alvin Toffler, *Learning for Tomorrow* (New York: Random House, 1974).
4. John McHale, *The Future of the Future* (New York: Braziller, 1969).

Chapter 1

1. Ralph White and Ronald Lippitt, *Autocracy and Democracy: An Experimental Inquiry* (Westport, Conn.: Greenwood Press, 1960).
2. Ronald Lippitt, Jeanne Watson, and Bruce Westley, *The Dynamics of Planned Change* (Westport, Conn.: Harcourt, Brace & World, 1958).
3. Edward B. Lindaman and Ronald O. Lippitt, *Choosing the Future You Prefer* (Ann Arbor, Mich.: Human Resource Development Associates of Ann Arbor, 1979).

Chapter 3

1. Lewis Mumford, *The Myth of the Machine: Technics and Human Development* (New York: Harcourt, Brace, & Jovanovich, 1967).

219

2. William Bridges, *Transitions: Making Sense of Life's Changes* (Reading, Mass.: Addison-Wesley, 1980).
3. Elizabeth Kubler-Ross, *On Death and Dying* (New York: Macmillan, 1969).

Chapter 5

1. Louis Raths, Harmin Merrill, and Sidney Simon, *Values and Teaching* (Columbus, Ohio: Merrill, 1966). Sidney Simon, Leland Howe, and Howard Kirshenabaum, *Values Clarification* (New York: Hart, 1972).

Chapter 9

1. Kurt Lewin, *Field Theory in Social Science* (New York: Harper & Brothers, 1951).

Chapter 11

1. Albert Ellis, *Disputing Irrational Beliefs* (New York: Institute for Rational Living, 1974).

Chapter 13

1. *Southgate Sentinel,* Downriver, Michigan, 1986.

Chapter 14

1. Richard Beckard and Reuben T. Harris, *Organizational Transitions: Managing Complex Change* (Reading, Mass.: Addison-Wesley, 1977), p. 25.
2. William Bridges, *Transitions: Making Sense of Life's Changes* (Reading, Mass.: Addison-Wesley, 1980). Figure 14.1 is adapted from this work.

Chapter 15

1. Robert W. Jacobs, *Real Time Strategic Change* (San Francisco: Berrett-Koehler, 1994).

Chapter 16

1. Discussed in Ralph White and Ronald Lippitt, *Autocracy and Democracy: An Experimental Inquiry* (Westport, Conn.: Greenwood Press, 1960).
2. This model was conceived in partnership with some colleagues convened for the task of creating a new model for organizations that would be appropriate for the context of whole-systems thinking: C. Cooper, R. Belz, C. O'Brien, and L. Scully.
3. This list of basic human needs was summarized by Peggy Lippitt in a survey of the major schools and theorists in psychology.

Chapter 17

1. Deepak Chopra, *Quantum Healing: Exploring the Frontiers of Mind/Body Medicine* (New York: Bantam Books, 1989).
2. Michael Talbot, *The Holographic Universe* (New York: HarperCollins, 1991).
3. Robert Rosenthal and Lenore Jacobson, *Pygmalion in the Classroom* (New York: Holt, Rinehart & Winston, 1968).
4. This model emerged during a workshop where colleague Jeff Bolanger and I were exploring a process I call Directed Energy and Preferred Futuring with other participants to create future states of health.
5. Sanaya Roman, *Living with Joy* (Tiburon, Calif.: Kramer, 1986).
6. For example, see Gary Zukav, *The Seat of the Soul* (New York: Fireside, Simon & Schuster, 1989).
7. Stephen R. Covey, *The Seven Habits of Highly Effective People* (New York: Simon & Schuster, 1989), and *Principle-Centered Leadership* (New York: Simon & Schuster, 1992).
8. George Land and Beth Jarman, *Break Point and Beyond: Mastering the Future Today* (New York: Harper Business, 1992).
9. Kay Gilley, *Leading from the Heart: Choosing Courage over Fear in the Workplace* (Boston: Butterworth & Heinemmann, 1996).

Index

A

Action goals: formation of, 79–80; and intention, 77; and setting criteria, 79; translation of future vision to, 77–78; two-phase process of translation to, 78–80

Action plan: enhancement tools for, 93–95; and first step action planning, 88–91; and first step rehearsal agenda, 91–93; and force field analysis, 86–88; and force field exhibit, 87; and gap between future vision and action goals, 82–83; internal dialogue and support tool for, 94–95; production of, 84–86; stages of, 83; and strategy development, 93–94; tips for, 96–97; tools for production of, 86–93; exhibit for, 90

Action planning exhibit, 90

Anti-Semitism, 15

Apollo Space Craft, 17

B

Basho, 61

Brainstorming, rules for, 43

Break point, 204

Breakthrough goals, 4

Bridges, W., 34

Brilliant, A., 98

C

Change: acting for, 99–101; change in perception of, 17–18; four basic human responses to, 18; and larger groups; 16–17, three stages of, 16, 17

Change agents, 16–17

Change model: components of, 151–152; definition of, 150; implementation of, 152–153

Change theory, 16–17

Choosing the Future You Prefer (Lindaman and Lippitt), 19, 87n

Chopra, D., 192, 193

City of the Year Award, 29

Communities: different approach for, 131–132; example of preferred futuring in, 141–147; and future sampler meeting, 132–135; and multiple preferred futuring sessions, 139–140; optional tools for, 136–137; and preferred futures scenarios conference; preferred futuring in, 131–149; and role of documentation, 135–136; and start-up conference, 137–139; tips for preferred futuring in, 147–148

Conflict, productive use of, 164–166

Consequences, scanning for, 42

Continuous scanning, 108

Core values, scanning for, 56–57

About the Author

LAWRENCE L. LIPPITT, PH.D., grew up in the group dynamics movement, spending every summer of his childhood and youth at the National Training laboratories (NTL) in Bethel, Maine, with the founders of the field. Around the kitchen table and in living rooms and meeting rooms, he listened, watched, and talked with his father, Ron Lippitt, and colleagues such as Ken Benne, Leland Bradford, Kurt Lewin, "Doc" Cartwright, Al Zander, Rensis Likert, and many others. At age 16 he participated in the first ever teen T-Group (the core group dynamics training methodology developed, researched, and offered at NTL, now called Human Interaction Laboratories), and by his early 20s he was a group dynamics expert.

While at the University of Michigan, Larry participated in the birth and development of the field of Organization Development, and he helped establish the first Organization Development graduate program there in 1967. During this time he learned Preferred Futuring from his father, who developed this process with Dr. Ed Lindaman, scientist and futurist at NASA. In the 1970s, as director of the Small Group and Organization Studies Program at Kent State University, Larry continued to teach the principles of Preferred Futuring and to use it with his clients.

For over twenty years Larry has helped large and small companies (including Fortune 500 companies), cities, counties, nonprofits, educational and government organizations, and individual teams—both nationally and internationally—build pathways to the future using Preferred Futuring. A certified teacher of the foundations and methods of Vajrayana Buddhism, Larry is developing Preferred Futuring for the next century by integrating Eastern psychology and Western behavioral science to explain the role of spirit and human energy in Preferred Futuring and large system change.

As president of Lippitt·Carter Consulting and cofounder of the Preferred Futuring Network, Larry facilitates whole system change for organizations and leads public workshops for all who want to construct a vision of their preferred future and mobilize the human energy to get there.